THRIVE

How to Achieve and Sustain High-level Career Success

by

Dean Williams and Mike Tinmouth

Grosvenor House
Publishing Limited

This book is published by
Grosvenor House Publishing Ltd
Link House
140 The Broadway, Tolworth, Surrey, Kt6 7Ht.
www.grosvenorhousepublishing.co.uk

A CIP record for this book
is available from the British Library

ISBN 978-1-78623-803-0

ABOUT THE AUTHORS

DEAN WILLIAMS

Acclaimed in the UK's Sunday Times newspaper for global business coaching, and recipient of 'The UK's Finest in HR And Talent Training Award 2016', courtesy of the HR Excellence Awards 2016, Dean is best known for combining his passion for working alongside Directors and Senior Managers, with his other entrepreneurial interests and work with a leading international charity. Dean is a regular columnist for a wide-variety of business press and entrepreneurial publications and author of the book *Creating Grade 'A' Business Relationships*. Dean is also a co-Founder of The Business Coaching Academy, which he set up to educate and enlighten managers and leaders on the art of coaching.

The majority of Dean's time is allocated to working with executives and boards offering them one to one and team coaching, as well as career counselling and mentoring. Dean boasts a client list that includes several global blue-chip corporations – Samsung, HSBC, Barclays, MasterCard, Avis Budget Group and BUPA to name but a few.

MIKE TINMOUTH

Mike is a journalist, public relations and digital marketing director who has featured in media outlets including the *BBC*, *Sky News*, *The Guardian*, *Forbes* and *Reuters*.

His career has seen him work with global corporates including Vodafone, WPP, Microsoft and IBM as well as fast-growing technology start-ups, including, Head of PR and Social Media at Azimo the online social money transfer service, which is backed by a $20m Series B investment round.

Mike holds a Bachelor of Laws degree and a Masters in Corporate Risk Management, with a particular focus on perception and reputation management. He combines his writing and academic interests, with his role as an advisor to several start-ups and publications.

ACKNOWLEDGEMENTS

DEAN

To my wife Roz for her unwavering support, encouragement, love and for just being the person she is…

To my clients who have contributed more than they think to this book!

To Mike (my co-author), awesome – a really enjoyable journey!

MIKE

To Jamie, Neil and Mum – my heart felt thanks for your support and putting up with me disappearing for days on end while burning the midnight oil – we got there together!

To Dean and Roz – another project completed – business partners, good friends and now co-authors!

CONTENTS

PREFACE

WHY THRIVE?

We wrote *THRIVE* with the intention of providing a shot in the arm for those individuals who are looking to progress their career to director-level and beyond.

To put it simply – we believe that those aspiring individuals, who are after continued sustainable career success, will take a big step to achieving their ambitions if they read this book.

So why, should we expect intelligent, ambitious individuals to invest their money but more importantly their time into reading this book?

The answer is a simple one; between us we have over 30 years of experience working across the private and public sector, from advising director-level executives at some of the world's largest global corporations such as HSBC, Barclays, Samsung, Tesco and BUPA to working side by side with startup entrepreneurs.

In the five years that we have worked together we have published over 50 articles on business and leadership and featured in publications from *The Sunday Times*, to *Forbes*, *The Guardian* and the *BBC.*

Thrive, is built upon a foundation of this successful hands-on experience. In the early chapters of the book we introduce the 'career annulus', a tool that will provide you with a tried and tested approach to achieving senior career success and later the skills needed to sustain and even surpass your career ambitions.

With a million or more business books available in print and digital, *THRIVE* attempts to be different. Whilst we touch on aspects of leadership and inspiration, this book has been written to give you immediate actionable insights wherever you are in your career. ***The structure of the book allows you to 'plug in and play' wherever you want to start, rather than following a traditional linear reading approach.***

With a plethora of job titles and expressions used to define top leadership positions across different industries, regions and cultures (titles and expressions meaning different things to different people), we use the language: directors, executives, senior-level executives, senior leaders and leaders not to confuse, but rather to 'connect' with the reader from their perspective. Be in no doubt that all of these terms are referring to the step up to top leadership positions.

Nuggets of information are summarized at the end of each section for ease of reference and have been handpicked from our personal experiences, from primary and secondary research and from the wise words of exceptional peers and business leaders – many of whom we have worked with.

Some of the ideas we share in this book will seem common sense or even obvious. Trust us when we say that there is no harm in positive re-enforcement; common sense is also not always as common as you may think. Our objective of this book is to make your behaviour and approach conscious. We believe that the consistency of message and re-enforcement throughout the book helps aid conscious thought.

While we will share stories of success, keep in mind that equally as many of the insights that we share come from the stories of those who have failed.

While a career setback can impact anyone and failure is nothing to be ashamed of, it is also something best avoided. Most of those failures we hear about are down to individuals who make the wrong decisions – notably they fail to plan a path to success.

And that is why we are sharing this roadmap – because we know that the knowledge, process and spirit of *THRIVE* works.

We have used it time and again to guide ambitious managers like you, to support their development and help them reach their goals.

By picking up this book (thank you!) you clearly feel there could be something in this for you. Keep your motivation and allow us to help you find some answers to your questions.

We're going to start by exploring with you the current business landscape – the realities of the current professional world that we are required to navigate.

Enjoy!

SECTION 1

THE PRICE OF ENTRY

CHAPTER 1

HOW LEADERS THRIVE IN TIMES OF CHANGE

The world is changing.

It always has and always will.

What makes the past nine years since the start of the global financial crisis so different, is the pace, scale and uncertainty of that change.

In less than a decade, we have seen the disappearance of the 'job for life.' Hoping that things won't change and that everything will be all right isn't a strategy.

The lessons we have learned, from the collapse of Lehman Brothers and the European banking crisis are that businesses and people need to better understand and manage risk.

We can no longer stand still and expect to go with the flow.

To remain relevant, we all need to be better prepared and have the skills and know-how to continually evolve and adapt.

If we don't take personal responsibility for managing and negating the impact of that change, then we risk being left behind.

Needless to say, it's an exciting, but also a challenging time.

So what's fuelling this period of uncertainty? The answer unsurprisingly is lots of things; ongoing global economic instability, political conflict, the rapid consumerization of technology, tighter regulation and changing employee expectations to name but a few.

But periods of instability create opportunity and not just downside risk. As big corporations like HP and Kodak flounder and fail, they are replaced by innovative and dynamic start-ups like Instagram – acquired by Facebook, just 18 months after it launched for $1 billion.

We live in a world where small businesses make up over 95% of all companies – yet where eight out of 10 will fail, usually within the first two years. In these businesses, founders, directors and employees are kept on their toes – they understand the game – ongoing risk and uncertainty means adapting or failing.

Talented businesses, like talented employees, scale and grow. Let's not forget that Walt Disney, MTV, CNN, Microsoft and over half the Dow Jones Industrial Average were founded during times of recession.

Businesses built during times of hardship are often more resilient. And that is largely down to one thing – leadership.

So, why then are so few talented managers making the most of this opportunity to grow their careers? Why do so many still subscribe to the 'job for life' or the 'I'll sit back and see where the journey takes me' philosophy?

Innovative products and genuine leadership find a way to succeed and indeed *THRIVE* during adversity.

It's about taking charge and accepting responsibility.

But most employees choose to stay put during a recession – they play it safe. And who can blame them? As Maslow's Hierarchy of Needs (opposite on page 5), demonstrates – job security is part of the key to human happiness (for most at least).

While millennials may rank company culture, flexible working, collaboration, engagement and vision and values as the most important factors in their career decisions, for most employees certainty, stability and a salary that pays the bills are the overriding consideration. The '*safety of employment*' often overrides their desire for opportunity and development.

Maslow's Hierarchy of Needs

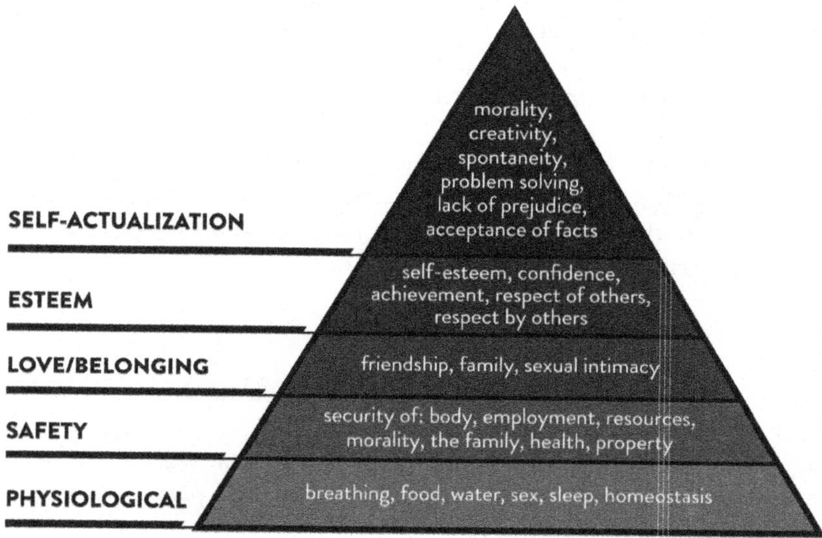

Figure 1: Maslow's Hierarchy of Needs, Psychology Review (1943)

Some have of course taken risks and seized the opportunities created during this period of uncertainty. And, as the economy shows signs of recovery, so those who have shown consistent excellence in performance and leadership will find themselves in greater demand.

CHANGING SKILLS FOR CHANGING TIMES

Over the past two decades, we have seen the skill-set of senior employees change to meet the demands of the new economy.

Gone are the days of reactionary leadership.

Todays' director level executives are taking a front seat in the development of the overall business strategy. They are innovative thinkers, with a strategic outlook; an entrepreneurial mind-set and they deliver transparent and ethical management.

Across every organization we see change.

No longer does a human resources (HR) director simply oversee payroll and recruitment. Today they own the organizations strategic talent agenda – recruiting, developing and retaining a world-class team. Successful businesses understand that having the best people working for you is no longer a nice-to-have.

Likewise, the Chief Technology Officer (CTO) is no longer the person you call when your email or printer doesn't work. Now they are responsible for developing and implementing complex strategic technology and communication infrastructure projects across the entire business.

It's not come easy. The change has been rapid, and many individuals and organizations have struggled in an increasingly competitive global talent marketplace.

As we will go on to discuss in this book, those individuals and organizations that are succeeding are those who have planned and invested in both their immediate and long-term futures.

As employees, our increased investment in terms of time and energy brings higher expectations – we've begun to expect more from the organizations we work for. We are seeking working environments that not only stimulate us, offer opportunities for personal and professional development but also those that allow us to work how, where and when we want. We are looking for roles and organizations that allow us to *THRIVE.*

The keywords for those aspiring to director level roles are no longer just – leadership, performance and profit. They are also now about inspiring, communicating and conveying the organizations vision.

When we sat down in late 2015 to write this book, a third (37%) of employees in the UK had left their last role to advance their career because of a lack of progression opportunities in their current organization.

That's a lot of people who have demonstrated that they have the ambition to further develop their career but feel they needed to move on in order to achieve that progression.

That churn of aspirational people costs employers time, knowledge and money while for the employee it means a period of flux and uncertainty within their personal and professional lives.

Through the process that we have developed and that we discuss throughout this book, we aim to share with you pragmatic advice that will enable you to take responsibility for investing in and managing your career ambitions.

By empowering you to best fulfil your potential in an environment where you both contribute and in return feel valued, this book will enable you to grow your career and sustain that success into the future.

MOVING FROM BEING A MANAGER TO A LEADER

Senior executives are no longer specialists.

Of course, many come from specialist roles, with unique skill-sets and knowledge, but in order to take a seat at the top table of your organization you now need a broader understanding of how the entire business works.

You'll never become CEO if you just think like an accountant or a marketing director. It just doesn't happen anymore.

A decade ago, managers in corporates led larger teams than they do today – teams who were more focused on fewer tasks. Now technology has increased our access to information, enhanced our productivity and at the same time increased demand upon dwindling resources.

The layers of an organization in which average employees used to be able to hide are being stripped away. Leadership is a far tougher task in this new world that is faster moving, more transparent and more complex than at any time in history.

Todays' senior leaders have an increasingly greater exposure to a bigger and broader breadth of roles and expectations upon them. Managing a department in a corporate organization has become much more like being the MD of a small business or a start-up founder – they have to have their finger on the pulse across the business.

While traditional routes to the top still frequently come from a technical or financial background, leaders identify early on, the need to engage with other departments in order to develop the broad width of knowledge required to lead complicated organizations.

We will go on to discuss why a broad exposure to your organization is fundamental to gaining access to the greatest number of senior decision makers and how to exploit (or should I say leverage!) those relationships.

In Chapter 8 we will explore in greater detail the skills, behaviours and character traits of leaders. The emphasis of developing from a manager to a leader is very much on future focus – helping you develop the knowledge and skills to not only achieve promotion but to provide you with sustained success.

A logical starting point for most people is, therefore, understanding where they fit in and what the career opportunities are within their current organization.

But there is a personal obstacle to overcome – your tolerance for the status quo.

In order to thrive you need to challenge the current thinking – continuing to do what you are doing is never enough.

The greatest impediment to career success is comfort.

Like anything, a comfort zone, within moderation isn't necessarily a bad thing.

We all need space or activities in which we feel confident and secure – these often allow us to explore new opportunities and ideas.

However, those who choose to live their lives within their comfort zone are significantly limiting their potential career radius.

So, you want to become a director? Are you thinking and acting like one in expectation of that next step?

The answer is that most managers struggle to identify the differences between what they do in their current role and those of a director – many feel they are doing most of the job already. Of course, not all directors are good at what they do, but more likely is that middle managers don't invest enough time into understanding the strategic importance of a leadership role.

Most of us are doers and not leaders. And here in lies a challenge – you may believe the ability to roll up your sleeves and get stuck in is a sign of dedication, a can-do attitude and being connected to the grass-roots. But senior executives need to demonstrate much more.

Today 80% of line-managers say that they have had to learn more and develop faster than they did five years ago in order to succeed, yet only 43% have a clear career roadmap in place.

WHEN SHOULD YOU START PLANNING FOR SENIOR CAREER PROGRESSION?

"Careers are like sharks, they need to keep moving, or they die." Ian Pearman, CEO of BBDO

Like people, companies come in all shapes and sizes and with all manner of routes to the top.

It's worth noting that the roles and titles of managers and executives rarely align within organizations or sectors. While the roles of 'Directors', 'Vice Presidents' and 'Managing Directors' may have many different meanings and seniority, most industries have a clear path to leadership positions.

Public sector organizations and government departments, for instance, are probably the most formulaic in terms of roles and hierarchy – but even these lines have become increasing blurred by the trend towards using management consultants in senior administrative roles.

Compare that to the non-profit sector where you don't follow a traditional career path to become a senior executive or CEO. While most countries are introducing greater governance requirements for the charitable sector, individuals are still primarily attracted to roles in the sector based upon passion and unique skill-sets as opposed to formal career progression.

We're often asked does age matter? Well, yes and no. While just a number, your age and career stage can affect your tolerance for risk. In our experience, the consequences of failure are broadly speaking lower the younger you are.

From an HR perspective, age is a leadership wild card – do you go for energy or wisdom?

Director level promotions are therefore more about earning the right to start having senior conversations – if your performance doesn't match your ambition, then you need to look long and hard at whether you have what it takes.

While the economic crisis of the early 1990s, the dotcom crash of 2000 and the global financial downturn of 2007 are fresh in many minds

– millennials know no different. Those individuals leaving college or university today have spent most of their adult lives living in a recession, saddled with debt and fully aware they may never be able to afford to buy their own home.

To young people, risk is ubiquitous; people are retiring later, and fewer young people are being recruited. While age and experience often equate to increased risk-aversion, young people are not bound by the failings of previous generations.

They perceive risk differently, without the constraints of a mortgage, children and fear of failure. The average millennial is now expected to change jobs every two years, meaning today's university graduates will have between 15–20 jobs during their life.

In an age of technology where entrepreneurs are building businesses in their teens, there's no right or wrong answer to the age debate. But what is fair to say, is that as you get older so you build assets and your risk tolerance shifts.

In many companies, you may start out life as an assistant, before hopefully making the step up to become a junior manager and then director. By your mid-40s, as a high flier in your industry, you may have progressed to a more senior director or even be in a C-Suite level leadership position. Take for example Ursula Burns of Xerox who started with the company as a summer intern in 1980 and over the next thirty years rose to become the first female African-American CEO of a major US corporate.

In the United States, CEO's in the biggest corporations are entering offices at younger ages. In 1995 the average starting age was 50.4 years but had dropped to 48.8 by 2001. In the UK, the average age of Chief Executive's is 53, while a Chairman is 64.

Even though it can take years, (in Ursula Burn's case 30 years) to make it to the top, the stay is often brief. 72% of the corporate CEOs in the US have held their positions for less than five years, with an average of just three.

Beyond the C-suite, there is a global trend towards smaller boardrooms, with a greater emphasis on non-executive directors. As requirements for corporate governance grow, boards now consist primarily of the chief executive, finance director and fewer but better-qualified and more highly rewarded non-execs.

So when should you start planning? Well, the answer is that there is no better time than the present! Success, however, only comes when you are completely ready and prepared for the challenge. The real question is… are you ready?

THE LANDSCAPE OF YOUR ORGANIZATIONAL TALENT AGENDA

The *Right Management Report* found that 74% of private sector companies and 93% of public sector organizations have undergone some form of restructuring during the five years to 2014 – largely as a result of the changing economic and commercial environment following the global financial crisis.

Uncertainty is the new status quo. This phase of organizational change has created new ways of working but also new conflicts, where individual intentions and business vision, are working against each other.

The response from companies to this uncertainty has been mixed.

Just 40% of respondents say they have introduced new HR measures in response to this continued period of change and upheaval. That is despite just one in four (24%) line managers seeing themselves at their current organization in a more senior role in five years' time.

What we're seeing is a major potential leadership gap emerging. For eight out of 10 of businesses, getting the best people is considered critical to their success, but far fewer have identified talent as a key organizational risk.

Consider for a moment *'how your organization would manage if its top performers all suddenly upped and left to join your biggest competitor?'*

Despite the importance that businesses place on people – talent management as a risk sits worryingly far further down risk assessments. In fact it currently sits below technology and on par with a natural disaster, despite the risk of flooding or a hurricane strike being far less likely than the best people leaving!

If you're an HR executive reading this, then take note. If you're an aspiring director reading this, then there may be a reason to be worried – your company may be telling you how important you are to the business, but they actually may not be doing a great deal to keep you from leaving.

According to the Report, companies that have taken steps to engage their employees have developed tools to better manage productivity including:

- improved flexible working arrangements (49%);
- increased internal communications from leadership to maintain morale (42%) and;
- promotions but with minimal pay rises (36%).

The days of big bonuses and incentives to stay at a business are largely something of the past. The employment market may be hotting-up but cash is no longer strictly king.

The future workforce will be fundamentally different from that which we see today –HR decision-makers are unanimous in the changes they expect to see over the next five years:

- More workers will opt to work part-time rather than retire resulting in an ageing workforce with fewer director level roles opening up.
- HR teams will face more opportunities and challenges of managing that older workforce.
- Individuals will begin maintaining and developing skill-sets in multiple simultaneous careers.
- More than half of all workers will be temporary or in contract or freelance positions.

But these are just stats and predictions – do they make a difference? Well yes, the working environment you know now will be fundamentally different by the time you may be making your next career decision. If you're to maximize your opportunities, you need to understand and stay ahead of the curve.

The result of these shifts in the shape of our workforce is that human resources expect to see the way in which companies manage people and in particular talent change:

- 72% of HR leaders and 59% of line managers say they will only be willing to invest in talent management if an employee is expected to stay at least a year.
- Most think that data and analytics software rather than more traditional methods will guide how they hire, engage and develop their workforce.
- Three-quarters think that most HR admin tasks will be outsourced.

- Over half believe that the future senior leaders of 2018 and beyond will be promoted from within their organization.
- 70% see future leadership teams being younger than the current leadership team and two-thirds see women taking up, at least, half of these roles.

Times of uncertainty have many different impacts on how organizations manage people. Whether it is cutting back on staff numbers, identifying and filling skills gaps, or managing employee fatigue, here are some of the key talent conflicts that professionals will be exploring:

- An ageing workforce working part-time or as consultants versus the expectation that the next generation of leaders will be developed internally from within the company talent pool.
- Leadership teams that become seen as more reliant on freelance consultants, contractors and external service providers in an attempt to control costs and increase productivity versus a visible, engaged and dynamic senior leadership who are able to communicate the company vision and drive growth.
- Employees who feel limited within their roles and future growth opportunities who are disconnected from their senior leadership team versus the need for a more agile and nimble workforce that is motivated to perform in order to create growth in the business.
- A lack of succession planning or a clear company talent strategy versus the expectation that managers will work with human resources on succession planning to develop the next generation of leaders across the business.
- Increased career fragmentation for individuals who feel unable to grow within their current organization versus the need for a clear company talent strategy that fosters internal leadership development.

The chasm between company and employee expectation has created a number of challenges for organizations – challenges (and therefore, opportunities) which every employee should be aware of and which can be exploited as you seek to manage your career progression.

YOUR PERSONAL TALENT AGENDA

Our hands-on experience and research, tells us that most people are perfectly satisfied with their current career trajectory.

Ambition isn't essential in life, and it certainly isn't for everyone.

Many people make a significant impact on the success of their organization without ever wishing to lead teams or progress upwards.

Some people have no desire to take on additional responsibilities and risk. Others are content in the expectation that loyalty and longevity will bring progression.

Of course, this is totally fine – climbing the ladder is not for everyone.

There are lessons and tools in the pages that follow (and the Big 5 Points at the end of each section) that will help most readers in achieving personal career fulfilment, but that isn't the focus of this book.

Taken from our opening preface:

We wrote THRIVE *with the intention of providing a shot in the arm for those individuals who are looking to accelerate their career to director level and beyond.* THRIVE, *is built upon a foundation of this successful hands-on experience. In the early chapters of the book, we introduce the 'career annulus' (on page 18), a tool that will provide you with a tried and tested approach to achieving senior career success and later the skills needed to sustain and even surpass your career ambitions.*

The focus of THRIVE *is to support those business managers who want to become leaders – those who are investing in their futures and have the ability to lead profitable departments, business units and organizations.*

We will approach managing your personal ambition by helping you to:

- identify your personal ambition
- understand the language of leaders
- state your career ambition
- develop your case for promotion
- deal with success and failure
- build sustainable career success.

THRIVE is intended as a guide and point of reference, not a one-off read. By the time you've finished with us we expect you to have a better understanding of your personal ambition and an actionable roadmap that helps you achieve your objectives.

Let us introduce our 'Career Annulus' © Dean Williams 2016 (see over on page 18)

Annulus in geometry means the area between a pair of concentric circles working towards a focused centralised objective – in this instance our focus on sustainable career development.

Throughout this book, we will be breaking down the component parts of the career annulus.

At the heart of our career annulus is 'price of entry.' An entry-level requirement if you like – have you earned the right to talk career promotion?

The truth is you don't have the right to 'sell yourself' unless you are already nailing it! Nailing it in terms of your current objectives, key performance indicators, and behaviours against company values. What do your performance reviews suggest? What is the quality of the feedback you are receiving? What is your truth? Not nailing it – do not pass go!

Every person reading this book will find themselves at a different stage in their career.

Some readers may be able to successfully implement the advice and roadmap (what we call the career annulus) contained within this book, and be ready to launch their career push within a few months.

Most can expect it to take between one and two years. And for some, it may mean starting from scratch, and following our guidance as you build everything from the foundation up.

Or maybe you're only just setting out on your career – in which case the advice we share can set you on the path to understanding how you will outperform your peers and scale the ladder faster than you'd previously imagined possible.

Career Annulus

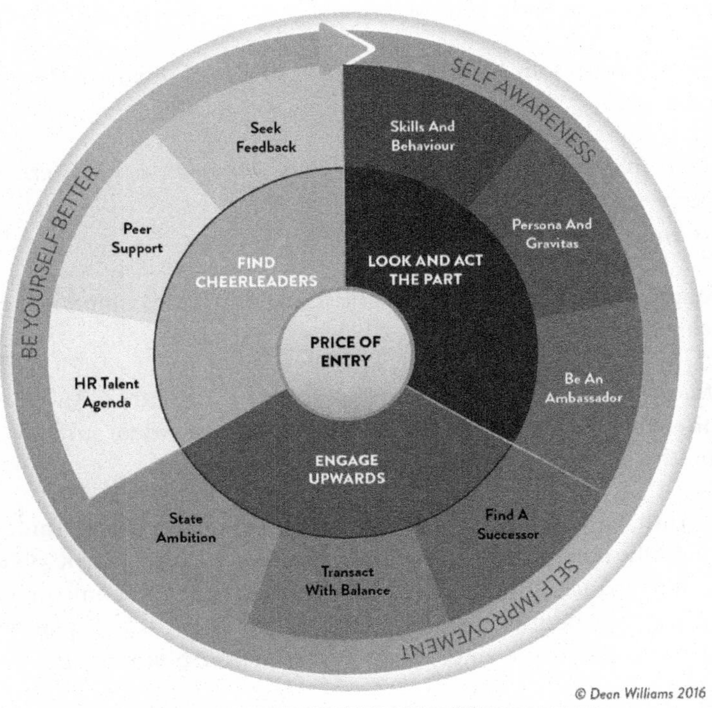

THE FUNDAMENTALS:

- Earn the right to talk promotion
- Deliver results
- Smash your KPI's
- Exceed expectations of you
- Let others see that you are ready for promotion
- Sell yourself and your quality to others
- Find supporters who actively promote your talent

Figure 2: The Career Annulus – Dean Williams (2016). Thrive

We will help you to understand the importance of self-awareness, self-improvement and sustainable development. But most importantly we'll help you understand the steps and considerations that are involved in knowing when you are absolutely ready for your next career move.

If you are feeling comfortable with this challenge, then it may be a sign that you are ready!

ARE YOU READY TO CONSIDER A PROMOTION?

Successful organizations require a dynamic workforce with multiple competencies to remain competitive in the increasingly global economy.

With talent management closely aligned to business success, you need to understand what your next promotion would entail and whether you are in fact both capable of progressing and ready for the next stage in your career.

Remember, winning promotion won't make you smarter nor any better at your job – you need to already be excelling if you are to stand any chance of succeeding and sustaining success in your new role.

It is worth considering what value can you bring to the business, and how the new role will impact your personal and professional life.

Far too many people think that simply because they have been in the business for an extended period of time, (and have proved effective at what they currently do) it means they are somehow entitled to a promotion.

But as we touched on earlier – managing and leading are two entirely different things.

Director level roles are focused on the strategy, while as a manager you are focused on executing the strategy.

There are certain questions you need to ask yourself that will indicate whether you are professionally and personally ready, as well as the tell-tale warning signs, that now may not quite be the right time to make the push for promotion.

The following are nine key characteristics that talent management teams will look at when deciding whether you are professionally ready (many of which fall within the 'price of entry' at the heart of the career annulus). Through the rest of the book we will reflect on these characteristics in readiness for making the push for promotion:

1. Are you excelling in your current role and do your results reflect this performance? As importantly, do your peers, managers, HR and the CEO know who you are and recognize your achievements?

2. Are you considered internally and externally as a thought leader and expert in your field?
3. Do you consistently motivate and challenge those around you to excel, while displaying emotional and conversational intelligence in all aspects of your role?
4. Does your performance and conduct consistently reflect the vision and culture of the organization?
5. Do you tackle tough challenges and decisions in a timely, transparent and accountable way?
6. Are you able to demonstrate versatility with knowledge of departments and strategies across the whole business?
7. Are you ready, committed and motivated to work harder, longer, and smarter than ever before?
8. Does your manager and organization regularly turn to you for solutions to pressing problems or nominate you as their spokesperson?
9. Do you have the personal and professional network in place to support you during the challenging and exciting times ahead?

In chapters four to 10, we will discuss how to position yourself to ensure you can place a tick in the box alongside all nine of these characteristics.

Next, it's about whether you personally, in your home, in your physical and mental world are in the right place to commit to not only winning promotion, but also to creating ongoing sustainable success.

Remember that getting promoted is often the easy part – continually excelling requires exponentially excellent performance. Every time you raise the performance bar, so expectations on you increase.

You should constantly be asking yourself whether you are giving yourself the best chance to succeed:

1. Does your appearance and body language reflect your level of professionalism and ambition?
2. Do you regularly talk about your leadership and experience outside of the workplace?
3. Are you an upbeat, energetic, and optimistic person with high energy levels?
4. Do you have the support of family and friends who are committed to helping you thrive?

5. Is your work/life balance in sync? Do you make sufficient time in your schedule for your family and friends and just as importantly, for yourself?
6. Do you eat a balanced and healthy diet designed to boost your energy levels?
7. Do you make time for regular exercise and monitor your diet and sleep? Do you get enough sleep that you are able to perform consistently all year round?
8. Do you avoid negative people and engaging in negative conversations?

It is amazing just how many people think that success is purely built upon hard work.

Don't get us wrong; hard work is critical, but so is planning, preparation and balance. The more confident and balanced you are, the more energetic and focused you will be.

The other thing people often forget is that getting promoted isn't a one-man show – it's not just about you! As the saying goes *"no man (or woman) is an island"* – you consistently need support from others to achieve your objectives.

This starts with your family and friends and builds up to the relationships you foster with key influencers in your organization.

Your 'support network' is there to help guide your decision-making at every step of the journey.

SECTION 1

BIG FIVE TIPS

1. The business world is changing as is the expectation of those in senior level positions.
2. You need more that specialism to be a leader.
3. Your 'price of entry' is key in determining your opportunity to talk up promotion.
4. Assess your readiness for senior promotion. Assess the whole you – is it in harmony with your other life elements?
5. Understanding the landscape of your organization's talent agenda is fundamental.

SECTION 2

ENGAGE UPWARDS

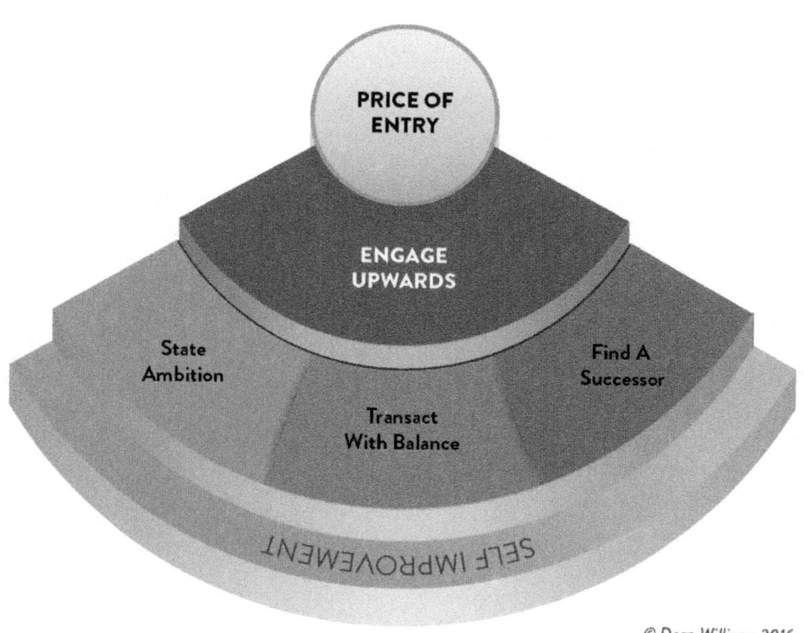

CHAPTER 2
STATING YOUR AMBITION

WHAT IS YOUR AMBITION?

"*Feeling confident – or pretending that you feel confident – is necessary to reach for opportunities. It's a cliché, but opportunities are rarely offered; they're seized.*" Sheryl Sandberg, Facebook

We've all heard the expression, "*you can do anything you put your mind to.*" But as we've discussed in the opening chapter, not everyone has the same levels of ambition – and that's fine.

Ambition isn't just about the hours you work but rather about fulfilment and a sense of purpose – regardless of how that is achieved.

For ambitious managers, the tenure in each role is on average a cycle of two, three or five years maximum. If you're not moving in these cycles, then you may be left behind and are increasingly less likely to be promoted.

If you're not being promoted, it means someone else is.

But, at the same time, few words have become as polarizing and double-edged as 'ambition', and that's a worrying trend. Most individuals define success in their professional careers based upon achieving the level of ambition in terms of job position, job satisfaction, legacy and remuneration.

Yes, there are those who see ambition as an extension of their ego – but for the rest of us, it's about pushing our abilities and capabilities to achieve more in work and life.

It's important to be sure that the ambition you hold is your own ambition and not what you believe other people expect of you.

As an example, I was recently working with a Head of Sales, an individual who truly loved their role.

During an informal meeting with the Managing Director, the MD mentioned that he envisaged my client rising to Director of Sales in future. My client was then informed by the MD of the ambition they had for him!

Rather than energizing the individual it caused him discomfort. He enjoyed working with customers, pitching to clients and being hands on (all expectations within his current role). Whilst a great tribute to his ability, his bosses opinion of his talent and ambition exceeded his own.

Those individuals who proclaim to have none, or limited ambition can be just as happy – and, in fact, live longer.

A study by the University of Notre Dame found that ambition can help you achieve success in things such as career, salaries, material wealth and education. But it is not always linked to long-term happiness or life expectancy, particularly when your ambition fails to translate to career success.

It sounds like a stark warning but later in this chapter we will talk in more detail about the importance of correctly timing your push for promotion – the Notre Dame research should be reason enough for getting it right!

It's no surprise then that people are being driven by a work/life balance rather than career ambition; partly because they want to start living a more balanced life now, rather than waiting until they retire.

When considering your current job role and whether it represents the right level of ambition, attainment and remuneration; there are some key questions to ask yourself:

- Does it fulfil you? Do you feel a sense of achievement and satisfaction in your current role and if not, do you have a clear idea of what satisfaction looks like?
- Are you working in a growing organization or corporate structure? Is there opportunity for short and long-term career growth with your current employer?
- What is different about your role? What is the difference between the role you are currently in, and the role you want to progress too. What are the key skill sets required for this role and is it achievable?
- Where are your critical path gaps? In order to achieve the position of choice, what is the most effective path? This role may not be your next position, and it may take planning and time to achieve it, as such what skills will you need to develop over time to get there?
- What is the timescale? Rarely will an individual's ambition stop at the next rung up the company ladder; whilst achieving promotion is an immediate aim, it is not an end objective. Plot your path to that position and develop a realistic timetable and roadmap for achieving it.

So, what then is the level of your career ambition and how far do you want to progress?

Too often, talented individuals become bogged down and focused on attaining the next role, rather than understanding the bigger picture – where does this next role enable you to go and what does it enable you to do?

If you are a senior leader wanting to progress you need to recognize that there are steps and planning involved – often in the form of a three to five-year plan.

You need to own your future and be able to mentally break down your career path and ensure consistency of messaging. The next role is simply the next step and not where you necessarily ultimately want to be.

Most importantly of all, ambition is nothing without action and execution. If you don't act in a purposeful way to fulfil your ambition, then you will find it to be a major limitation on your personal happiness, sense of achievement and a longer-term hindrance to your career.

WHAT TO DO WHEN YOUR CAREER FEELS OUT OF YOUR CONTROL

"Inspirational and revolutionary thoughts are seldom born from stagnation." Jan Osburn

Most things in your career are entirely within your control.

But not all career moves are planned, nor are they all vertical – this, however, doesn't mean you cannot exert some degree of control.

Redundancies happen – unemployment rates in the UK and US soared during the recession.

Big corporations went bust. Iconic brands like Blockbuster and Borders disappeared from the High-Street. Talented people lost their jobs overnight.

Adversity requires decisive action, and we'll talk later in Chapter 12 about dealing with failure and difficult decisions in more detail. Needless to say, the prospect of redundancy is never pleasant – but it is a reason to ensure you have a clear proactive career roadmap in place.

It's equally true to say that career moves can come from a number of unexpected paths; through a merger or acquisition, through talent placements or secondment or even through pivoting away from your current trajectory altogether.

Like we've said time and time again, planning is key. People who feel confident about their skills and abilities find it easier to make career shifts.

Both a merger and acquisition will see a duplication of back office functions. Mergers enable an employer to pull together and keep their best talent, while with acquisitions, the larger firms absorbs the smaller and first in, last out is the general rule.

In 2014, Microsoft's acquisition of Nokia saw 18,000 job cuts or 14 percent of the overall staff as it looked to 're-balance' its workforce – the largest round of lay-offs in tech industry history.

While big corporations often acquire competitors to establish their market dominance, more often they are smaller 'talent acquisitions' aimed at securing the best people in the industry. Most of Facebook's acquisitions have been 'talent acquisitions' with CEO Mark Zuckerberg saying in 2012, *"we have not once bought a company for the company. We buy companies to get excellent people... In order to have a really entrepreneurial culture one of the key things is to make sure we're recruiting the best people. One of the ways to do this is to focus on acquiring great companies with great founders."*

When businesses combine, there are usually job losses – and managers, directors and even CEOs are not immune. But those employees with the most knowledge and relevant skills often remain. This may lead to opportunity, with an expansion in your role or even a promotion in a much larger company.

While unexpected change is rarely easy, being prepared for an uncertain future can help. You always have more control than you might think. So, what should you do if your career progression suddenly feels like it is out of your control?

- If a merger, acquisition or even downsizing is being talked about, look at where the potential growth and weakness areas are for the business and the relevant skills you can bring.
- Speak with your manager or CEO to establish if you will have a role within the new or re-balanced organization and develop a plan.
- If you see opportunities, then articulate your desire to remain and contribute to the organizations' growth.
- Work with your manager or HR team to map out a potential new role – or begin the process of looking for a new job.
- You will usually have around six months to prepare yourself. Use each month wisely to achieve another step in your plan, starting with reviewing and updating your current job description and CV. From there, following many of the steps set out in this book will help you on the process to greater self-improvement and career possibilities.

To re-iterate, you always have more control than you might think.

Those at the top will be focused on developing the wider macro-level strategy for the new look organization, but that doesn't mean you can't influence the potential impact upon your own department and career.

WHY MISTIMING YOUR NEXT STEP CAN BE CAREER SUICIDE

There's a Chinese proverb that, "*the best time to plant a tree is 20 years ago. The second best time is now.*"

Once you've understood your ambition and established whether you are ready for a promotion – then comes the big decision – when do you start?

Remember that once you state and share your ambition, you're stuck – you are in it for the long haul. Key stakeholders will remember what you stated – an expectation of motivation has been created!

Career progression is a risky business – particularly as we've already established that you are excelling in your current role. Why give up the safety of what you're already doing?

Risk is personal in so much as it is down to individual perception – what you perceive to be a risk is likely to be different from the person sat next to you.

But taking risks in your career is important when the positive upside outweighs the possible negatives. If you are talented and ambitious – staying where you are is not an option. Machiavelli summed it up when he said, "*all courses of action are risky, so prudence is not in avoiding danger (it's impossible), but calculating risk and acting decisively.*"

Even if you are content with where you are in life remember that in today's economy if you don't keep pace with change – you risk becoming irrelevant in the ever-changing workplace.

Never make assumptions about your career – nothing should be left to chance.

A decade ago if you worked in the public sector or a big corporation like Microsoft or HP, then you effectively had a de facto job for life. That world no longer exists.

Many highly talented individuals start out on their careers as superstars but struggle to sustain early successes.

Hard work and results go hand in hand. By attempting to state your ambitions for a director level role before proving yourself (without a 'price of entry'), you risk not being taken seriously, and you undermine how everyone around you perceives you.

If you are not thriving in your current role then harbouring delusions of self-importance or blindly believing that you would somehow perform better in a more high-powered role will leave you exposed to potentially fatal career risks.

We've discussed in Chapter 1, some of the characteristics that say you're ready for a career jump – but what are the warning signs if you are not?

- If you are not excelling in your current role, then you need to have courage and clarity of mind to realize that something needs to change. That might be the decision to refocus your energies on getting things right where you are or alternatively reassess your career path.
- Do you suffer from fear about the next step of your career? Nerves are to be expected, but fear and anxiety are telltale signs that you are not emotionally ready for the challenges ahead.
- Are you at risk of appearing like a career hopper? Ambition and progression fit side by side, but it takes time to master any new role. If you've only recently been promoted, then it's unlikely you've had time to truly demonstrate learning, growth and value. Starting to talk about your next job too early can be seen as a sign of a lack of focus.
- If you do not enjoy your current job, then it's time to reconsider your career path and the organization you work for. If you don't wake up early every Monday morning excited about the opportunities in store for the week ahead – you're going to struggle to succeed long-term in the business.
- Do you have an excellent working relationship with your peers and senior stakeholders in the organization and do they rate you? Take a step back and consider how they would score your work performance on a scale of 1 to 10 and the type of feedback they would provide.
- Making the step up to a senior executive will bring new challenges from day one. Yes we all need time to adjust, and there is an element of on the job learning to do, but if you don't already have a clear understanding of the role you wish to progress into then it is time to go back to step one of this process and do your homework. Failing to plan is planning to fail.
- Winning your dream promotion is a fantastic achievement but from day one you will be expected to perform at a higher level than you

have done before. If you are already finding your workload or work environment stressful, then be warned of the inevitable pressures and ongoing scrutiny that you will find yourself under.

- Have you successfully managed and delivered a significant organizational project? Volunteering for or being chosen to lead business critical projects are the clearest opportunities to test and showcase your leadership skills to senior influencers. Without such evidence of achievements, you're unlikely to stand out from the crowd.

Career progression involves calculated risks – but success comes with a holistic understanding of the organization, the expectations of key influencers and a high degree of self-awareness.

We live in an age where we all expect things immediately – technology has transformed our access to everything from information to consumer goods so much so that we've become increasingly and often irrationally impatient.

Taking risks for the sake of it is simply foolishness, as every career move comes with a chance of failure.

It is, therefore, important that you don't leave anything to chance. Analyze opportunities and your readiness and consider both the upside outcomes should you be successful, but also the downside implications if you fail.

HOW SHOULD YOU GO ABOUT STATING YOUR CAREER AMBITION?

Many candidates, especially internal ones, believe they are a shoo-in for a role or a promotion. This attitude of entitlement is one of the biggest obstacles that leads to failure.

To succeed you need to consistently demonstrate your worth to the organization, as well as showing that, you understand the skills you bring to the role and why these are more beneficial than your competition.

Thus, the first step is admitting to yourself that you are ambitious – understanding the level of that ambition and planning for success.

This self-awareness is also important because every time you talk about your achievements and ambitions, you will be reminding yourself of your objectives – that reinforcement is an important part of ensuring you achieve them.

Communicating your ambition to your line manager and other senior decision makers is critical – these individuals have the power to shape your career.

Regardless of the esteem in which you hold them, one thing is for sure; they are not mind readers.

Asking their advice on how they achieved success and on recommended routes to a promotion are all ways to highlight your desire to progress.

Communication and articulation are both intrinsically linked to emotional awareness. Pushing your promotion credentials does not mean you have to belittle or diminish someone else's suitability for the role.

Nor do you need to suddenly transform into the 'teachers pet'.

But you have to consistently remind people of your successes – remembering that your conduct and achievements must echo the impression of readiness that you are trying to give.

So how do you avoid overstating your ambition?

Formal documentation and performance reviews such as appraisals are one way.

Alternatively, you can discuss your career directly with your line manager or CEO, particularly about the opportunities available for future development and the breadth of projects or responsibilities that can set you on the path to that promotion.

As a guide, here are some of the key areas to consider to help others engage with your ambition:

- Set personal goals as part of you organizations formal appraisal process. Whether it is your line manager, HR team or CEO that conducts performance reviews, this is the perfect opportunity to state your ambitions and goals for the year ahead.
- Use those formal or informal job reviews with stakeholders to discuss skills you wish to acquire or projects/tasks you would like to undertake as a pathway to future promotion. Be clear and concise about what it is you are asking for and your end objective, which is to gain further skills to enable future promotion.
- Most appraisal or review meetings require employees to provide written feedback on their performance and personal development. This is an ideal opportunity to always provide a detailed focus on your recent performance and results. You can set yourself targets for the next quarter or half, based upon your desire to ready yourself for further progression.
- As discussed earlier, engaging with your organizations' talent agenda, be it training and development opportunities or a more formal request to join a talent pool are essential. Working alongside HR is a great way to enhance your skills, but also to become better known within other departments in the organization.
- Be proactive about volunteering for key tasks and projects. Being seen to have the confidence to tackle challenging tasks demonstrates self-confidence in your own abilities. The larger the scale of the project the more senior stakeholders are likely to be involved and, therefore, the more of an impression you can make. But note – failing on the big stage could have catastrophic consequences, so pick your targets carefully.

It's also not necessary to broadcast your ambition to the whole world, but the more confidants and stakeholders that are aware – the more people will put you front of mind when opportunities or conversations arise.

> Be warned! The following is advice I gave to an ambitious client recently, helping her build her resilience in the face of perceived jealousy from her peers.
>
> Often others can feel exposed by those that show high levels of ambition – that's their problem, not yours. It is not a reason to lose ambition – it's a reality check and something to accept.
>
> Get comfortable with the discomfort. Do understand that ambition isn't for everyone!

If you still feel that you are not getting noticed, then speak to your boss about what you need to improve. Enabling yourself to perform better and deliver your results means it's also easier for your boss to be confident in giving you a promotion – confidently communicating your ambitions is a win-win situation.

THE IMPORTANCE OF CONSISTENCY OF LANGUAGE AND BODY LANGUAGE

When it comes to earning a promotion, your results should speak for themselves. But while no one ever likes a show-off, it is important that you consistently highlight your leadership qualities, your responsibilities and most importantly achievements.

This may sound a little egotistical, but it's not. It's about striking the right tone (in terms of confidence in your own abilities) in such a way as to inspire confidence in those who have the power to promote you.

Being able to manage the conversation in such a way is in itself a key leadership skill. The ability to converse at an executive level and dare I say 'manipulate' the conversation is a key skill – both in written and verbal forms.

This self-confidence and self-belief are about the persona that you build for yourself and the way in which you hold an air of authority. Once you've made your ambition known it is important to understand that you are being watched by everyone – your peers, juniors and boss. An expectation has been created!

Feedback on your performance can come from anywhere at anytime – never forget you are being watched and judged more than you think.

This is particularly the case in formal settings such as presentations and meetings. Ambitious individuals cannot be passive. They must always strive to control conversations and make memorable interventions.

It goes without saying that you need to prepare for meetings and understand the subject matter – your interventions should always be considered and made in a way that raises the quality of the discussion.

You must also take every opportunity to add value. This can involve anything from arriving with your insights on latest available market data, right through to summarizing or circulating additional information after the meeting to support your position.

The language used by leaders sets them apart from their subordinates. Those wanting to get a seat on the top table should heed the following:

- Focus on the positive value you bring to an organization, both in meetings and conversations.
- It is important to be specific about your objectives or analysis, but also flexible in reacting to alternative views or in taking up new challenges.
- You must retain your ambition, but also, ensure you are always realistic about what is deliverable.
- Talk about your professional, rather that personal ambitions and objectives. Your employer will give you a promotion if it is in their business interests to do so, not because they want to pander to your ego.
- Make sure you are consistently conveying your accomplishments and the financial value that you have brought to the organization; as in sales or financial efficiency savings made.
- Understand your market value – are you a star performer just within your organization or when assessed with the whole industry or sector. Benchmark yourself!
- Do you have the mind-set of a business leader? Do you avoid negativity, and talk in terms of solutions and vision (and consistently deliver)? This mind-set includes how you manage feedback in a way that helps you grow and improve yourself.
- Do you look like, and act like you are already a senior leader – dressed appropriately, punctual, well prepared, confident, committed and clear in your views?

As important as what you say, is the way in which you act and present yourself.

Do you conduct yourself in the way an executive would?

Consider whether your conduct mirrors that of your boss or other senior influencers in the organization.

In the past, it has related to dress code, but in recent years, there's no doubt dress codes have become more relaxed. The way you dress will not guarantee success, but turning up like you've just rolled out of bed will cast doubts on your professionalism.

Of course, if you're working in a tech startup, jeans and a hoodie may be the standard office attire but as a rule of thumb, you should be dressing for the job you are aspiring to, not the one you're already in.

As we'll go on to discuss in Chapter 7, we are living in an age when in-person interactions are increasingly on the decline and that makes first impressions that much more important.

Body language plays an important part in first impressions and longer-term how you are perceived. It's important to consider the impact of body language—and simple nuances in your positioning can impact on people's opinion of you. There has been a great deal written on the subject, but some of the basic points are:

- A hunched or 'small' body position can again convey the sense that you are intimidated, lacking confidence or uncertain. Instead, consider a more expansive body position, upright with hands by your side. This more positive positioning conveys success and confidence.
- Focus is key. People who are easily distracted by looking at their phones, watches or notes can appear disinterested in the conversation. Instead, focus on interacting and engaging, asking questions and providing insightful interventions on areas where you know your stuff.
- It is as important to respect an individuals' personal space as much as it is to ensure that you convey warmth and interest.
- Avoid unnecessary movements such as continually readjusting your chair, face touching, chewing on your pen, tapping the desk or re-adjusting your notes. These movements are all associated with both nervousness and disinterest, so make sure you limit your body movements and keep your hands still.
- It's the old piece of advice in business, make eye contact with people you are talking too – as a guide, this should be about 50–60% of the time you are interacting with them. Eye contact says a lot about your emotional intelligence such as respect, confidence, warmth and honesty.
- It is remarkable just how many people fail to smile when they are introducing themselves. Experience of hundreds, if not thousands of interviews over the years tells us that nine out of ten people look miserable when they walk into a new introduction – especially job interviews. Yes, you may be nervous but nothing gives off a bad vibe quite like someone who looks like they don't want to be there.
- It used to be just a guy thing, but a confident meaningful handshake tells you a lot about a person regardless of gender. A good guide is to always look to match the firmness of the other persons grip and to be confident and authentic.

Communicating your ambition ultimately comes down to understanding your audience and environment, their expectations and beliefs and then presenting yourself and your views in a way in which instils confidence and belief in your ability to get the job done.

In the following chapters we will discuss more about managing your upward progression, the mind-set of a leader and developing your emotional intelligence – critical aspects in how you present and convey yourself and your message.

CHAPTER 3

TRANSACT WITH BALANCE

UNDERSTANDING HOW TO TRANSACT WITH BALANCE

"Leadership is not a position or title, it is action and example"

Leaders are made, not born.

Of course, many leaders, across all walks of life, are inspired to take control by the example of others, but the decision to act is ultimately theirs alone. Even reluctant leaders take responsibility.

For those aspiring to the next level in their career, you will be judged by the actions you take and the example you set. We talk about developing not only the ability but also the awareness to *'transact with balance'*.

Transacting with balance is about your ability and confidence to stand shoulder to shoulder with C-Level executives – understand how they perceive you and know how to act and behave in their presence.

While country HR teams drive talent strategy, in reality, it is the C-suite at a global level who control your future. Bosses use their authority and seniority to push a candidate they believe will deliver.

Being considered talented in your field will open the door, but being taken seriously by senior colleagues will be instrumental in your career development. If they don't have absolute faith in your ability to perform on the 'big stage' – they will not risk their own reputation on an unproven colleague.

Simply put, success in this area opens the door to a leadership position.

Being a leader is about what you do next; or rather, what you should already be actively starting to do, to confirm to your senior colleagues that you are ready to slip seamlessly into your next role.

Your success as a leader will be judged increasingly upon the performance of the team you manage. Your role shifts to supporting talent as opposed to demonstrating how you stand out from the crowd – that part will already have been achieved to get you where you are.

When we talk about transacting with balance, it's about demonstrating your readiness. As a guide consider the follow dos and don'ts:

Don't

- Come across as too demanding of senior colleagues time or attention. Avoid acting like a needy child – unless you want your boss treating you like a parent would!
- Be conscious to the fact that asking for feedback too regularly could suggest that you are not confident in your own abilities!
- Finding people you aspire to and building relationships with is one thing – but don't suck up too much! No one likes 'that' person!
- Self-confidence and communicating your achievements is critical but don't just self-promote! Sometimes you need to let your results speak for themselves.
- Be aware of office politics but don't over play the game!
- Never let your ambitions get in the way of you doing your current job well – just because you want to be seen to be transacting at a higher level doesn't mean you can afford to sacrifice on your current tasks. Remember always your 'price of entry.' Failure at the final hurdle could have lasting consequences.
- Demonstrating a 'can do' attitude is one-thing but trying to exert authority or push through projects simply to aid your profile is guaranteed to alienate and offend.

> We have seen countless people morph into 'child mode' when connecting with significant senior executives – becoming an unrecognizable version of themselves, poleaxed by fear of putting a foot wrong!

Do

- Ensure you add value to every business conversation. Being up to date on the very latest company and industry data and having your own opinion will ensure you have at least one memorable contribution to make in every meeting.
- Work on your intellectual USP (Unique Selling Point). Develop a deeper understanding of an aspect of the business where you can be an authority. This will help give you an edge.
- Smile! If you know your stuff, then why not feel relaxed? Always appear confident, you being nervous risks making everyone else nervous too!
- You should always look and act like you deserve to be where you are. Day in and day out.
- You should understand what success looks like for you peers and manager and help them in reaching their goals.
- You should always bring a positive mental attitude – a 'can do' leader demonstrates to a team how to overcome challenges and make the most of opportunities.

Our careers are continually being shaped by those we meet, and by ourselves through our behaviour and attitude. Senior colleagues can stall your career progress, but they are also able to help in identifying your strengths, in developing your self-confidence, and in helping you push barriers.

If you are already transacting with senior executives on this level, then you are ready to have serious conversations about your ambition, skills and leadership abilities.

DO YOU HAVE THE MIND-SET OF A LEADER?

As we've discussed, leadership involves people and not just yourself. Your mind-set is about the attitudes and beliefs you state and the culture and performance expectations that you create within your team.

Your mind-set is closely linked to your ability to read situations and your resulting decisions and actions. It also dictates the type of working relationships and interactions you have. We divide people into two mind-sets – fixed and growth.

People with a fixed mind-set believe in their basic abilities such as intelligence and skills, whereas those with a growth mind-set focus more on the process that leads to success. Those with a growth mind-set see challenges as an opportunity and failure as part of the learning process.

People with a **fixed mind-set:**

- Try and forcibly convey their intelligence, as opposed to relying on results to demonstrate their abilities.
- Try to avoid challenging situations, which they perceive could undermine their success.
- Don't take constructive criticism or feedback well, viewing it as a personal attack on their abilities rather than being useful to their development.
- React to setbacks in a defensive manner, making excuses and pointing fingers.
- Can often feel threatened by the success of their peers and resent other peoples success.
- Are less likely to develop and achieve their full potential.

Those with a **growth mind-set:**

- Are more likely to seek out opportunities to learn and experience new things. They are committed to continued personal development.
- Embrace challenges and view them as a learning opportunity.
- Take on board criticism and use it to develop personally and to help develop their leadership skills and management techniques.
- Seek out aspirational high achievers and learn from the success of others, continually pushing themselves to achieve more.

- Find opportunities to mentor colleagues – not only helping their peers grow but at the same time developing their own skill sets.
- Have an entrepreneurial approach to identifying new opportunities and providing answers that solve problems.
- Have a global mind-set which gives them the ability and emotional intelligence to positively influence individuals around them regardless of background be it cultural, political, social or institutional.

Leadership positions are not for everyone.

So how do you know if you have a leadership mind-set? Well, one of the key drivers of mind-set is simply; do you come ALIVE when thinking of challenges?

Does thinking about opportunities and challenges allow you to dream about what you could achieve in that role? Have you thought about promotion not simply as a more important title and bigger salary, but rather have you plotted actionable deliverables you would bring to a project or role?

As we said at the outset of this chapter, leaders are made and not born. Just because the growth mentality doesn't come naturally, doesn't mean you aren't capable of being a leader. Often, a mentor or business coach will be best placed to help you manage your ambition. They are in an objective position whereby they can offer advice and guidance but the decision to engage must come from you.

A business coach or mentor is also not simply a one-on-one facilitator who works exclusively with you behind closed doors. They can help shape your mind-set, ask the questions within your organization regarding landscape and opportunities and help focus your preparation. They also help to provide clarity, and a reality check, offer feedback and drive performance.

Thinking like a leader and putting that mind-set into action are two different things. Some of the key behaviours of leaders are:

- They move beyond simply getting the job done to a more visionary mind-set identifying where future growth and opportunity will come from.

- The ability to simplify, effectively communicate and lead the organizations visions, values and objectives to individuals at all levels, both internal and external.
- Knowing what they want and how to get their team to implement those objectives. They are able to delegate work and responsibility while at the same time retaining knowledge of key projects.
- They have a mind-set that responsibility sits with them.
- They realize that 80% of results come from 20% of activities. They understand that their time is better focused on managing people than projects.
- They actively plan to plan.
- They make decisive, sharp, intelligent decisions.
- They motivate and inspire those around them.

We've all been back to a high school reunion or connected on LinkedIn with a former colleague and thought to ourselves – 'I was certain that so-and-so was going to be a lot more successful than they have turned out.' They may simply have lacked the ambition to progress in their careers, or they may have been weighed down with a fixed mind-set – fearful of leaving their comfort zone and thus failing to seize the opportunities to fully achieve their full potential.

Those individuals who THRIVE identify where the gaps and opportunities are within the organization and fill them.

DO YOUR RESULTS GIVE YOU PERMISSION TO DISCUSS PROMOTION?

"*You can't build a reputation on what you are going to do.*" Henry Ford

Deserving a promotion and getting one are two very different things.

By now you know that communicating your ambition is key – does your performance in your current role give you the right to even discuss a promotion?

Put simply, far too many managers are obsessed with promotion and titles as a means to enhance their own CV's when they have not yet proved themselves where they are.

While your educational background can be important, it isn't critical – no MBA will get you a seat at the top table if you aren't as good as you think.

Too often individuals are concerned with whether they have sufficient technical skills – in reality you wouldn't be where you are without them. When it comes to leaders, organizations 'hire character and train skill.'

If you are not exceeding expectations in your current role, then no one will have confidence in you succeeding in a more senior position.

Stories about your success are not enough. It is down to cold hard figures.

Most organizations will have a list of five to seven key competencies they expect of an individual. It is not just about meeting the required standard – but exceeding it. These are in place in big organizations as a guide to what to expect. You must be able to articulate how you exceed these in a way that inspires and demands follow-up discussions and sets the foundation for discussions about your future career progression.

If you are unsure of what is expected of you, then go and have the right conversations at the right level – give yourself the best chance to succeed. Go and ask your boss what his or her expectations of you are.

It is never too late to turn any situation around. Objectives can be poorly set and, therefore, you have to ensure you clearly manage them and are not defined by someone else's unclear objectives.

There can be no excuses for under performance. You are intelligent enough to set your own objectives and push yourself into the zone.

One way to set your objectives is by using Key Performance Indicators (KPIs). These are not simply a metric used to measure business performance but rather an indicator of direction and achievement.

Simply put a KPI is, "*an actionable scorecard that keeps your strategy on track. They enable you to manage, control, and achieve desired business results.*"

KPIs should:

- Correlate and communicate the organizations vision.
- Have senior management buy-in.
- Be easy to understand and initiate.
- Lead to direct action and results.

They are vital in helping leaders understand whether they are meeting objectives and where additional focus is required. Successful leaders understand what these KPIs mean across the whole business.

It is important to understand all the KPIs of your role, including the silent ones:

- Have you received the recognition in your current role that you think you deserve?
- Do you have sufficient credibility and gravitas within the organization?
- Have you created a professional persona?
- Do colleagues warm to you on a personal 'human' level?
- Are your already delivering exceptional results?
- Have you demonstrated consistency throughout your current role?
- Are you confident in yourself and your ability?
- Have you shown a willingness to be adaptable and to stay the course?

- Have you demonstrated innovation and entrepreneurial thinking?
- Can you demonstrate P&L responsibility?

What can you do to get noticed and achieve your KPIs?

- Demonstrate a diverse knowledge, across the organization and industry (competitors, global market, etc.) by spending time on conversations across the organization in a way that leads to a change in perception of your role and expertise. Invest more time, reading about, researching, attending events and speaking with experts so that you gain a wider view and opinion about the business, beyond just what you are exposed to in your current role.
- Ensure you contribute at a senior level by working across different teams in the company and don't get pigeonholed into one type of role. Always seek to expand your experience by volunteering for special projects and taking opportunities to work with colleagues in different departments. Not only will this help you develop new skills but also become known to more colleagues.
- Demonstrate proven qualities that exceed the role you are in by continually pushing yourself further. Winning promotion is as much about proving you already have the necessary skill sets of a more senior position, than just being good at what you are already doing.
- Always show a willingness to seek feedback and act on constructive criticism – it's a key trait of leadership and demonstrates your ability to listen, adapt and develop.
- Understand the frameworks and processes of the organization and particular where you stand regarding the talent strategy. Are you on the radar of senior executives? If not, then what do you need to do to elevate your chances.
- Help build organizational capacity by motivating and challenging your subordinates by inspiring and promoting excellence. Become sought after as a thought leader – someone who can speak to teams and develop their understanding of a particular area of the business.
- Explore ways in which to own company internal and external communications in such a way that ensures you get noticed. Writing a blog, volunteering to speak at conferences, making contributions to company emails or working on company white papers are all ways to be seen and heard.
- Network internally and externally more effectively and keep track of who you have connected with across the organizational structure and

whether the next time you meet them, they actually remember who you are and what you do.

An example of creating positive headlines and recognition for yourself was with a senior Leadership and Development Partner in a Bank. She set about building a name for herself by creating the companies first recognition program. She created the objectives and then worked with internal and external stakeholders to get management buy-in.

The initial design and implementation of the project involved colleagues across every department and motivated colleagues by recognizing and rewarding exceptional performance. It received significant internal promotion, backed by the CEO. And because this individual was the first to propose and deliver on the project, she was recognized as the architect of the success. It also prevented anyone else from ever being able to claim they were first – she blocked competition by pioneering a new program and maximizing exposure to the full.

HOW WILL YOU KNOW IF YOU ARE SUCCEEDING?

If you are already performing at the level that the new job requires, then you have what it takes to at least discuss promotion.

Being selected to take part in the organizational talent program is a clear indication that you've been identified as a potential rising star – but that's where the hard work starts. In smaller organizations, being asked to work on complex or more diverse projects is usually a sign that management has trust in your abilities.

A good benchmark of the impact you are having is whether the projects you have worked on have succeeded. In the weeks and months after you've completed a task, are you still being recognized as having added value?

By this stage in your career you are also likely to have managed several teams already – are those teams still performing and have the staff you managed progressed in their own careers? Being a successful leader means that you have to create a legacy of success that survives long after you have moved on – teams that fall by the way-side are not evidence of long-term success.

Do your colleagues want to work with you on projects or as part of your current team? Success breeds success and talented managers attract individuals with equal ambitions who want to both learn but also benefit from being in the 'jet-stream' of an upwardly mobile leader.

Are colleagues excited about the prospect of you being promoted? Beyond simply being happy for your success, when the right people are promoted it reinforces trust amongst employees that the system works and that opportunities for progression are available for strong candidates.

Conversely, there are warning signs that you are not performing sufficiently and, therefore, are not ready for the next step. These include:

- Fear beyond the normal. While it's normal to be nervous or apprehensive, if the thought of moving into a more senior and more stressful role keeps you awake every night, then you are probably not emotionally ready for the commitment. Anxiety is fine and normal but needs to be controlled.

- Apathy is a career killer. If you're not enthused by the opportunity, you will never push yourself to achieve and therefore, never reach your full potential.
- A failure to clarify your own ambitions, once again reveals that you have not suitably considered or planned your next role or your longer-term career path.

As important as it is to be performing at the level of a senior leader, you must also be acting like one if you are to move seamlessly into the role.

CHAPTER 4

FIND A SUCCESSOR

WHY SUCCESSION PLANNING IS NOT JUST ABOUT THE CEO

When we talk about succession planning most people immediately think about C-Level talent management – preparing the next CEO for the task of leading the business.

It's time to change that.

Succession planning should never be an exercise that is reserved solely for senior leadership roles but instead should focus on ensuring continuity of leadership and knowledge across the organization at every level.

And that starts with developing a strategy for who will succeed you in your current role.

Your career success is dependent in part upon the strength of the talent within your team – they are both there to deliver results but also to continue your legacy.

Planning for your career future is not simply about you. Just because you are ready for a promotion, doesn't mean the business or your boss is ready for the disruption it would cause if they don't have a suitable candidate to replace you.

As a star-performer, you may find that you are so valuable to the business in your current role that they will struggle to fill your shoes.

It is your responsibility to nurture your successor and demonstrate to your boss and the wider business that they are also ready to progress.

It is important therefore that you stop and think about who it is that will be your successor? Very few people are truly irreplaceable, but the more senior and integral you are to the business, the bigger the impact your departure has, and therefore, more planning and preparation will be required.

The loss of a key member of the leadership team can have serious implications on knowledge transfer, business relationships and company culture – all of which hurt the bottom line.

This 'people change', while inevitable touches every stakeholder in your business from managers to employees, customers to competitors, suppliers and stakeholders.

Because of the enormous impact that loosing your best people (even if only internally to a new role) can have, leadership transition begins long before any roles become vacant.

A quick sporting analogy – great sporting coaches or managers like Sir Alex Ferguson of Manchester United or NFL legend Vince Lombardi continually reinvented teams, as key players (personnel) left – others were transitioned in, creating continued success for years.

As legendary business guru, Jim Collins describes it, getting "the right people on the bus," is critical – how you plan an exit from your current role will also reveal a lot about both your character and your effectiveness as a leader.

Talent gaps harm businesses, and it's your role as a manager to work with the HR department to both nurture internal candidates as well as hire new ones in a way that is aligned with the business strategy.

And it is that element of planning, in an environment of continually increasing competition for top talent that sets successful managers and organizations apart.

Twenty years ago it was easy to recruit a manager from a competitor, now it is both more challenging and more risky, placing an even greater emphasis on your internal talent pool.

Broadly speaking we focus on three types of succession planning;

- Strategic leader development, which is the on-going development of top talent against the organizations strategic vision (we'll discuss this in more detail in Chapter 5).
- Departure-defined succession whereby the organization is working towards a defined long-term timetable for employees leaving.
- Emergency succession to replace managers or senior leadership when they announce their sudden or unexpected departure.

These three processes are best managed by developing an on going talent management program that is aligned with the organizations strategic vision and incorporates the six key stages of succession planning, namely:

1. Ensure that you align your business and talent strategies to determine which roles, skills and talent are needed to deliver your business objectives in the short, medium and long-term.
2. Conduct a thorough talent assessment to identify current and future talent gaps and determine whether the internal talent pool is sufficiently ready to progress either via vertical or lateral advancement.
3. Where the talent assessment identifies immediate gaps, ensure you are able to recruit and develop a pipeline of top quality candidates to fill key positions.
4. Work with your staff on ongoing performance assessment, communicating effectively both the organizational strategy and how they align and contribute to the businesses success.
5. Understand your team's career ambitions and work with them to find opportunities to develop their skills, experience and exposure.
6. Understand what is important to retain and engage your top employees – be it rewards and remuneration, an exceptional company culture or through enabling the autonomy and flexibility in how they perform their job.

A successful succession plan maps the strategic landscape, identifies risk and prepares contingencies and, as a result, minimizes disruption to the business.

As former Procter and Gamble CEO A.G. Lafley described it, "If I get on a plane next week and it goes down, there'll be somebody in this seat the next morning".

Planning for success starts with your people.

Developing an effective succession plan requires a company culture where staff, at all levels of the business are encouraged to show strong leadership. With this core leadership philosophy running throughout your business, top to bottom, you reduce your dependency on a single manager or director and ensure continuity and smooth transition of knowledge and responsibility.

ASSESSING YOUR INTERNAL TALENT

Succession planning for your role is a means for the organization to ensure its continued effective performance when you step up or move on – who takes on your role will have an impact on your legacy and on how you are viewed both as a judge of talent and as a manager/coach.

In Chapter 5 we will discuss understanding the organizational talent agenda and how this impacts your progression from senior manager to director or C-Level executive. While these more senior roles are usually in larger organizations administered by the human resources department, when it comes to identifying and nurturing a successor for your own role you're likely to find yourself working largely on your own.

Yes, HR should and will play a part in the search and formal recruitment process, but most of the hard work is done months in advance by working with your team to develop your 'leadership bench'.

- What are the talent needs of the business over the next three to five years?
- What are the needs of my department or the project I lead over the next two to three years?
- Who within my team has consistently demonstrated the leadership skills to meet those needs?

It is not simply enough to have a 'favourite' or to anoint your successor – there needs to be transparency, rigour and fairness in the process in order to provide an equal playing field to anyone who may wish to be considered. Failing to do so will create disappointment, disharmony and division.

A good place to start is, therefore, to spend time learning about the business structure for promotions and ensure your team are aware of any immediate and future opportunities for progression, including what would be expected of them if they were one day to step into your role.

Look for individuals who align themselves with the organization's culture and values. Ensure that a detailed job description for your role is available to your team members, one that details not only roles and skills but also accountabilities and attitudes.

Work with members of your team to understand and challenge their ambitions and discuss with them what you view as their strengths and weaknesses.

It is always worth looking beyond what you would view as the 'quick fix' successor and instead work with those who display aptitude and enthusiasm who can be developed into a leader.

Consider the future structure of your department and whether team members would benefit from lateral moves working in other functions or teams to gain broader experience and exposure. Work with senior management and HR to also identify opportunities for mid-point promotions to roles such as a team leader or to manage a special project.

Allow those that express a desire and have shown sufficient ability to 'shadow' you for a time to gain better insights into your day-to-day role and where possible grant them exposure to senior meetings and the ability to participate in the decision-making process.

Keep detailed notes of candidates and score their performance and ability against the job description – measuring candidates not just against their colleagues but also against their peers at other firms, particularly your competitors.

Using a systematic evaluation process to identify, train and nurture individuals with the right attitude, personality, skills, knowledge and readiness is useful not only for your own decision-making but also when it comes to providing constructive feedback.

Consider following this seven step process for assessing your internal talent:

1. Identify the senior positions within your team and the skills and experience of the employees in those roles.
2. Compare their performance in key competencies against your own current job role and evaluate their results.
3. Provide opportunities for broader experience and training and development needs.
4. Evaluate how they are perceived by their peers, superiors and the wider organization.

5. Ensure that any potential candidate to be your successor is clearly seen by colleagues as such and is credible and respected.
6. Conduct a thorough assessment of the candidates desire and readiness to progress.
7. Make sure that you are ready and confident to hand over control to your successor and are clear on your desired timetable.

A critical part of the process is ensuring that the chosen candidate is ready to progress and can step near seamlessly into your role. While you should make yourself available for a thorough handover and future support you must be confident that they have the skills and gravitas to own the new position from day one.

Done well and your succession plan should not only ensure a successor who is ready to build and strengthen your legacy, but it should also leave you with a team or department where the best people are in all the right positions. A team, where everyone is clear and confident about their future, and the value they bring to the business.

HAVING HONEST CONVERSATIONS

As a leader/manager within your business, you carry an amazing influence over your direct reports and particularly over the culture within the organization. Handling succession planning is one of the clearest ways in which you wield influence – your words, actions and decisions can literally make or break careers.

How you communicate these decisions will have a lasting impact on your team and how they perceive you. The greater the level of emotional intelligence that you display, the greater the influence you have.

Your job is thus to use this influence to the maximum advantage of the organization – inspiring aspirational leaders to drive themselves forward, whilst also acting to rally those who fall or stumble along the way.

Delivering feedback is an essential skill for you as a manager – one which helps to reinforce leadership messages and given positively, to develop your team. Like with any core disciplines, some managers deliver feedback extremely well, getting the most from all their people, while others experience mixed results.

The key to consistent success is down to following defined processes and displaying certain behaviours about how we are going to deliver feedback. Are we going to just tell them ('push-style') or do we want them to tell us ('pull-style')?

Both are effective models– getting it right will result in an individual feeling motivated and determined to move forward even when we are giving developmental feedback.

The following models demonstrate perfect alignment with the 'push'/'pull' techniques;

The *BROFF feedback model* is focused on the 'Push' technique whereby you give clearly defined feedback – it is a more direct and less engaging style but it leaves less room for confusion or ambiguity.

Behaviour

- indicate the purpose of the feedback;
- identify the behaviour/action to be changed and give examples
- separate behaviour from personality; and
- have your facts to hand.

Reasons

- establish their view of the situation; and
- jointly explore the reasons underlying the current behaviour/action.

Outcomes

- discuss current outcome as a result of this behaviour/action.

Feelings

- elicit their thoughts/feelings on the current outcome and the need for change.

Future

- agree with the individual future actions – what they will do differently;
- discuss development needs;
- agree on measurables and review dates; and
- ask them to summarise future actions to confirm understanding.

When opting for the 'Pull' technique managers are reliant upon a more 360 approach to feedback, with the team member working to identify a development area as part of a discussion following an observation. The *SECS feedback model* demonstrates the 'Pull' technique:

Self-evaluation

- get the individual to comment on what they thought went well and why;
- what do they think could have gone better and why? and
- state your view on what they have identified and question further as appropriate – ensuring that biggest impact area has been flagged.

Effect

- get the individual to comment on what effect the current behaviour/action had – what consequences did it bring; and
- question further as appropriate until impact is understood.

Commitment

- elicit their desire to change current behaviour/action – get them to tell you the pay-off.

Solution

- agree with the individual how they will approach differently next time;
- agree a defined solution;
- discuss development needs;
- agree measurables and review dates; and
- ask them to summarise future actions to confirm understanding.

As a leader, part of your responsibility is as a coach to your people. Leaders work with their team to get the most out of them.

You are responsible for providing the environment and support mechanisms that enable your team to Thrive. You should continually be on the look out for those potential future leaders who show a desire for greater accountability and responsibility and then help those individuals develop and gain the exposure they need.

PROVIDING OPPORTUNITY AND MOTIVATION

Successful teams are diverse teams. They combine a balance of skills, experiences, people demographics and career ambition. As we've discussed already, not everyone shares the same levels of ambition, but competition for opportunities and progress exists within most teams and while healthy it also needs to be managed.

It goes without saying, that in the same way as you have your own career ambitions, so many of your team moving up the lower rungs of the ladder will have their own career aspiration and will be motivated by the desire to progress themselves.

It is important that every employee understands the succession process.

Many employees are continuously seeking opportunities and new challenges that will help them gain exposure within the business and develop their skills and capabilities.

A big part of your role is ensuring they get to participate in those projects in order to demonstrate their full abilities and that those projects or tasks are aligned with opportunities for reward and recognition, increased decision-making and cross-department working.

In most businesses it is down to you as the manager to share with your staff the opportunities available and the process and criteria on which candidates will be assessed. There is also a more personal conversation to be had with each individual as to which roles they may or may not be suitable for.

Ensuring that you create opportunities for individuals to shine is critical to ensuring you attract and retain the very best talent in your team and the business. Your direct reports continued success, is a direct reflection on your performance as their manager.

Done well, and your succession planning process will demonstrate that you are willing to commit the time and energy into investing in your staff. For any employee, this provides motivation that you are aware of and committed to their continued growth and development.

But with opportunity comes risk – for every opportunity to lead a new project or be promoted there are likely to be dozens of potential internal candidates, many who currently work together and will likely have to work closely together in future.

Disappointment is an inevitable part of the business world – for every company or individual who succeeds someone has no doubt come second. Problems start arising where disappointment turns into conflict and it is your role to manage internal competition for places in a positive way that channels your team's energy in to a creative force that benefits the business.

Part of the process of managing competition is to focus on clarity of communication but also ensure that everyone is given a fair opportunity to Thrive.

There are few greater killers of motivation and enthusiasm than nepotism. While we all undoubtedly harbour opinions about who would be best to fill our role once we vacate it, the final decision must be based on performance and not favouritism.

A single disappointed team member left unmanaged can have a toxic effect on a previously harmonious and successful high-performance unit. If left unresolved lingering conflict situations can often result in disillusionment and dissatisfaction and usually lead to that individual(s) feeling isolated from the team and from you as their manager.

But as with any 'risk-event' internal conflict can have positive outcomes if managed effectively.

Offering to provide extra support and guidance such as developing a growth plan can help people become a stronger candidate for future promotion gaps.

NURTURING EXPOSURE AT THE RIGHT TIME

A good departmental succession plan identifies the right structures, roles and skills that will be needed over the next three to five years.

As a long-term plan, it is an on going and evolving process of identifying, reviewing and developing talent to ensure leadership continuity for all key positions in your department.

Perhaps one of the most difficult aspects of talent management is balancing the timings of succession. You have your own ambitions to manage but at the same time, you need to coach and mentor your team until you are confident that they are ready to step up.

You need to nurture talent and ensure exposure at the right time, only once the candidate is capable and ready while at the same time realizing that ambitious employees have a desire to see rapid career and remuneration progression.

Promoting someone too quickly presents risks to both the business and to your reputation, not promoting quickly enough and you risk losing people to your competitors, after having already invested time, knowledge, relationships and money into developing them.

Like anything there are signs that a candidate is ready or not:

- Are their performance and results exceeding that of their peers?
- Are they comfortable, confident and enthusiastic when transacting at a higher level?
- Do they hold gravitas and authority in everything they do?
- Are they respected by their colleagues, peers and superiors?

One of the most effective ways of investing in retaining top talent is by focusing on relationships – talented staff are less likely to jump ship early if they feel they have begun to develop strategic relationships within the business.

Once you have identified your successor and agreed the future structure of the team that they will manage then work with them to develop a transition framework.

Planning a timetable of handover creates comfort and negates risk, ensuring that your team are bedded in and operating effectively long before you depart – helping, in turn, to ease your successor in and phase yourself out.

Once you are confident that your successor can successfully take the reign you can focus on ensuring that your team are stepping up.

At this point you should be focusing on higher value items, big projects, key reports and the type of work that will make you and the business famous.

Don't sweat the small stuff – that's what your handpicked and well-drilled team are there for.

You were once a star-performer, now your role is on demonstrating that you are a leader. Developing your team and your successor highlights your ability to manage and inspire people around you – doing so in a manner that engages and retains the most talented people in your department is a reflection of the influence you hold.

Remember that the ultimate achievement of a leader is to build a team that can thrive without you. Succession planning is about managing risk and ensuring the future success of the team/business.

It's critical that you are assured by your identified successors capabilities, behaviour and readiness to step up. It is equally critical that those assessing your future/promotion are assured also!

SECTION 2

BIG FIVE TIPS

1. Ensure your ambition is your own ambition and not an expectation from someone else.
2. You can plan your future – you are in control more than you think.
3. Stating your ambition carries an expectation of additional commitment, through the eyes of your superiors.
4. When transacting with your superiors avoid being tentative and needy.
5. Planning for your future is not simply about you – you need a strategy for your replacement.

SECTION 3

FIND CHEERLEADERS

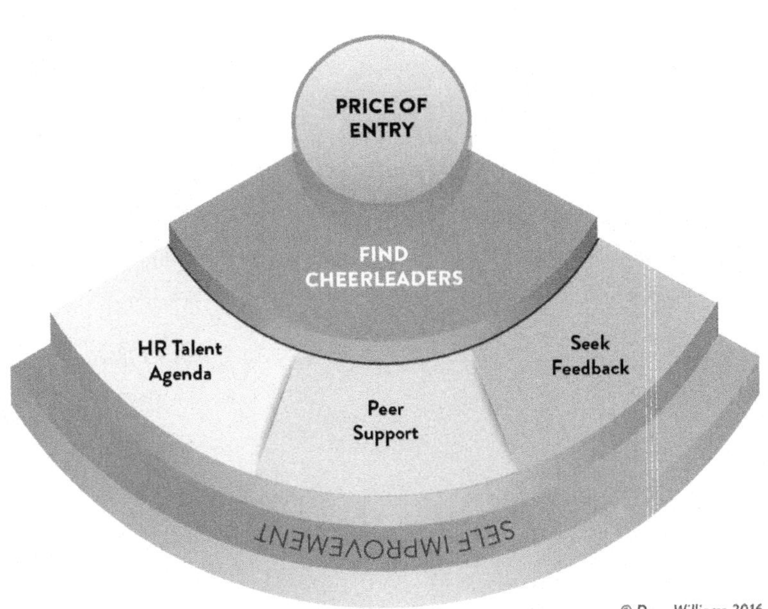

CHAPTER 5

THE HR TALENT AGENDA

THE IMPORTANCE OF UNDERSTANDING THE HR TALENT AGENDA

Being in a position to seize opportunities in your career requires a clear strategy. This particularly applies at the top of a business where it is critical to understand how your business approaches talent management (briefly touched on in Section 1) and who the key influencers are.

Consider it part of doing your homework – and remember that every organization is different.

We've included this chapter to give readers an appreciation of the process, as well as an insight into what HR and senior influencers expect from exceptional candidates. But whilst insights are there to stimulate your thinking, it is essential that you do your own research.

So what is talent management? Well, the Chartered Institute of Personnel Development (CIPD) defines talent management as:

"The systematic attraction, identification, development, engagement/retention and deployment of those individuals with high potential who are of particular value to an organization, either in view of their high potential for the future or because they are fulfilling business/operation-critical roles."

It has been 17 years now since McKinsey & Co published their ground-breaking report, '*The War for Talent*', which first flagged the long-term talent shortage brought about by globalization and an increasingly nomadic millennial generation.

Young people are today as likely to join a company based on purpose and vision, as salary and prestige. Part of the solution was the realization that businesses needed to better engage top talent within the organization and that growth will come from emerging markets, which are largely reliant on developing local human capital.

Engaging with your organizations talent management strategy is a great way to not only look to enhance your skills but also to work alongside HR executives in the business – people who will play an important part in both your development and in the decision as to whether or not you progress in your career.

Until the 1990s HR had often been considered an administrative function – leading process-oriented tasks that needed to be fulfilled in order to recruit, train, deploy and manage employees.

Suddenly there was the realization that top talent – alongside company culture – were vital sources of competitive advantage. Boards woke up to the fact that talented individuals were no longer bound to a single corporation their entire careers but were free to flow around a global ecosystem. The result was that HR decision-makers now needed a global and local vision and to align talent with the business objectives.

Ultimately it was the increasing complexity of global enterprises, the acceleration in technological advancement and an aging workforce that belatedly ensured that HR came to be recognized as being business critical – in the same way as technology, finance and risk.

The talent function now increasingly exists to help the business: know your people, grow your people, move your people – it is no longer an operational necessity, it is a strategic imperative.

There is little surprise then that the 2014 *Flux Report* found that 65% of senior HR executives expected to play an increased role in aligning HR strategy with business strategy over the next five-years. In particular, there's been a shift to managing senior executive positions, succession planning and critical posts across global organizations.

So what does success look like? Well there are many answers, but organizations that are continuing to thrive have adopted the following principals:

- World-class HR is recognized as being linked to business performance and success.
- They understand the risks of not investing in talent including risks to growth, succession, continuity and sustainability planning.
- Talent-management is not the sole responsibility of the HR department, but rather the CEO and the board play an important role in managing the company's talent pool.
- Processes for identifying top talent, including performance evaluations are based upon a rigorous data and results driven approach.
- The organization effectively communicates the importance of talent management both internally and externally in order to deliver a transparent working environment.
- Talent strategies are both theoretical and practical in their implementation.

One of the most striking factors in successful organizations is how personally engaged senior stakeholders are in the design and development of talent processes. While, ultimately it is the HR talent professionals who are judged upon the decisions and performance of appointees, the ongoing commitment and support to the program of the CEO, including mentoring executives is increasingly viewed as part of leadership legacy building.

Successful global organizations also create a clear link between the ambitions of the organization and the career paths and opportunities for top talent. They talk about 'talent mobility' – how career progression, succession planning, talent mapping and business strategy are integral to the success of people and organization.

They focus both on identifying key roles in the organization and ensuring there will be a pipeline of talent, as well as investing in individuals just because they are considered 'performers' and have 'high potential.'

The positive impact of effective talent management cannot be underestimated and can be felt across the organization, including:

- Increased engagement in the organizations vision by building a more inclusive culture that maximizes the value of every employees contribution.
- Clearer KPI setting, which results in increased productivity and delivery and more objectives being achieved.

- Nurturing top performers into senior leadership and executive roles.
- Enhancing brand image in the employment market with an increased ability to attract and hire top quality staff – employer branding.
- Identifying key talent gaps and evaluating options for addressing them and a more thorough approach to succession planning.
- Better Integration of new staff into existing teams.
- Creating mentorship and internal development opportunities with a high return on investment through targeted talent spend.
- Ensuring that the leadership of the organization is skilled and diverse.

The rapid growth of the internet over the past two decades also means that when we talk about globalization we're no longer limited to just large corporates – today SMEs and even start-ups are expanding globally at record pace. And, as companies continue to grow, so they will increasingly need talent from a wider breadth of backgrounds, with different experience and skills across both traditional and emerging job functions – the executive of the future will not simply come from the sales or finance department.

As well as new markets, a global business means new labour markets, where local knowledge and trust is key. For HR and talent managers, this creates new opportunities and challenges. The ability to be agile and responsive in deploying people across the organization is key to building highly skilled teams in culturally diverse regions – regions where trust is the currency of leadership.

So how then do organizations decide who makes it onto the talent agenda, and what can you do to better understand and engage with the process to enhance your chances?

HOW DO ORGANIZATIONS TRACK THEIR TOP TALENT?

You may be reading this book having already made your mind up to leave your current employer – but the reality is that most senior executive appointments come from within, and this trend is predicted to grow over the next five years.

Why? Because buying in talent is not sustainable and is inherent with problems.

Research suggests that external hires are 61% more likely to be fired from a new job than an internal candidate – largely because of the difficulty new recruits find in adapting to culture and processes of a new company.

When it comes to senior executives, it's a similar story – 86% of CEOs were appointed from within. And loyalty counts – in the US, 51% of CEOs have spent more than 20 years working for the company, while globally nearly 75% of CEOs had spent 35 years or more with the same company.

Hiring the 'unknown' can be a very expensive, disruptive and also a time-consuming process as you onboard new people and they take the time needed to build their network and integrate with the company culture.

In the perfect world, recruiters and headhunters would have a queue of exceptional applicants ready to fill each position. In reality, there is almost always a disconnect between the right candidate and the right opportunity or time.

Hiring from within retains loyalty and pride in the brand, increases motivation and engagement (as employees can see a career path), provides an extremely powerful retention and reward option and provides companies with an ability to 'grow their own' – i.e. nurturing and moulding people according to where they need the business to grow.

Retained talent will also have had extensive training and a certain degree of familiarity with the position. This helps individuals across the business develop their skill sets, resulting in higher performance and ensuring that you will have experienced and qualified executives in a position to assume leadership roles when required. Organizational talent pools thus provide both a reliable and tailored internal source of talent and a valuable piece of the succession planning process.

And by publically stating your commitment to an individual as a 'high-performer' you are also aiding in retaining that individual. It is obvious but worth repeating, every time an experienced manager leaves, you lose valuable knowledge but also potentially clients and other business relationships.

No matter how talented a new employee is it will take time for them to reach that level of knowledge. Retention affects the bottom line. Not only does it reduce recruitment costs, it also retains and grows business relationships.

According to the UK Civil Service HR practitioners guide:

"A talent strategy helps an organization to determine the skills, experience and capabilities required to deliver upon its strategic objectives. By reviewing your personnel and their roles you will start to see what you already have, what you will need to buy in, and what you need to develop to achieve your organizations' goals."

To identify future business leaders, businesses need to continually assess their key people through regular talent audits and one-on-one assessment sessions, such as personal performance and development reviews.

It requires a process to 'weigh and measure' people, deciding what high-potential looks like to the organization. HR professionals map this capability against future strategic objectives – thereby matching business and human capital requirements.

This talent 'mapping' by senior managers identifies key talent gaps as well as areas of strength.

The objective of this analytical approach is to enable the mapping, scoring, monitoring and reviewing of talent to ensure both a diverse workforce and one that has a proven track record of success.

For a business like Apple, being a technology front-runner means everyone wants to beat you. When you become one of the world's most valuable brands, sustaining growth and innovation is tough. Not only do they have to compete on creating great products, but also for talent in a sector dominated by younger workers. With the likes of Google and Facebook looking to recruit Apple's top engineers – Apple has found itself under sustained pressure.

Back in 2008, Steve Jobs created the foundation of Apple's talent success – the secretive 'Apple University', a manager-training program which Jobs was personally involved in shaping. The aim? To teach top-talent what it meant to be an Apple employee, embed the company's culture and history in the psyche of senior managers and ensure that the talent-pipeline remained loyal to his vision.

Whilst not everyone's organization has the budget to sustain their own 'university', failure to invest in these processes could mean losing current employees, their knowledge and skill sets, as well as wider damage to the perception of the brand as an employer of choice.

At technology giant Dell, employees and managers mutually create the employee-development plans. The process is reviewed annually, with ongoing feedback, coaching, training and on-the-job development.

Every quarter the Executive Leadership Team and Board of Directors at Dell conduct talent reviews specifically focussed on the context of the business strategy where they asses how to:

- develop talent imperatives;
- identify mission-critical jobs;
- forecast talent needs;
- assess and calibrate talent;
- identify development actions for top talent;
- report progress; and
- create succession plans.

When it comes to career progression all the evidence shows employees value regular feedback and reviews and that these are seen as an effective way to develop your skills, broaden networks and support your career planning. The opportunity to develop and broaden skills in different contexts not only benefits personal development, but also promotes valuable collaborations across the business.

The organizations that are succeeding are always on the look out for people who add value. These organizations are building their own talent pools of potential future leaders.

These individuals can come from anywhere. They may, like you, be an aspirational high achieving manager ready for their next career move. In smaller or medium size businesses, they could be someone your boss met at a company event, an early adopter of your product, a competitor from a rival firm, someone whom your customers recommend or simply a casual acquaintance they met at drinks at a friend's house.

Life in the formal and informal talent pools is tough – the key is for you to understand and get with your organization's talent agenda.

> We have seen on a number of occasions talented executives who have chanced their arm, backing just one senior C-suite relationship, ignoring the benefits of engagement in a prescribed organizational talent agenda. Success comes from managing both elements, not from taking a risk and ignoring one or the other.

But like anything, talent pools need to continually develop and evolve with time to meet the changing operational needs of the business.

Companies need to consider both the current needs of the business and the people or job-roles that are key to delivering immediate success. There is then the on-going challenge of aligning the HR and talent strategy with the medium to long-term business objectives – the type of people, skills and roles the business needs to achieve its future vision of growth and success.

Every organization has individuals with key skills that are central to its competitive advantage – skills that need to be retained and enhanced. Understanding the skills that set your business apart, help HR establish the talent pools the organization needs. From there they create a list of learning activities and on the job opportunities that support the development in each key area.

All in all, it's a tough job, as the organization needs a certain level of maturity to first see the benefit and then to follow through on a talent strategy – particularly as return on investment can often take some time to become apparent. Companies that have cracked it however will be far, far more competitive than their competition in the long run.

SINK OR SWIM IN THE TALENT POOL

"First get the right people on the bus (and the wrong people off the bus) and then figure out where to drive it." Jim Collins

Research from the CIPD into perceptions around the ownership of talent management found that overwhelmingly individuals believed it was their responsibility to take ownership of their own career and manage their own development.

Your personal commitment to learn and develop is paramount to your success.

Remember the golden rule – you only get out of it what you put in.

Respondents to the CIPD research also agreed that senior level support from within the business (be it the CEO or senior executives) was essential for ensuring long-term success.

Organizations have finally come to the realization that talent strategies cannot focus solely on just the top performers at the top of the organization. Instead, they focus on three types of employees:

- High-performers – those who are excelling in their current role.
- High-potential performers – those identified as having the potential and inclination to continue to develop with the organization.
- High impact employees – those who are most engaged and best represent your organization's vision and values.

Research by the CIPD found that 81% of employees taking part in talent programs and pools believed that participating had positively impacted their engagement at work, with 94% saying that it would help them develop their competence or leadership capabilities.

Once in the talent pool, continual development is key. Winners grow with the opportunities presented to them. You must be prepared to take on greater responsibilities in order to broaden your knowledge, skills and experience. Candidates are assigned projects and tasks, designed to stretch them and expose them to a range of functions across the business.

While different people learn and develop at different paces it's critical to manage your time wisely. Falling behind can cast a shadow on your prospects – failing to deliver on the warm-up to the biggest stage can prove fatal to your ambitions.

More so, being publicly recognized and part of something important while at the same time working on development skills and self-confidence are all important motivators.

Overwhelmingly, talent pool participants value what the exposure and access to senior C-suite executives enable, as well as opportunities to take part in a more diverse range of roles and to receive expert coaching and peer mentoring.

But life in the talent pool isn't always easy.

By its very nature you are now surrounded by the best of the best. If, you thought that standing out from the crowd was difficult in your team or department – imagine what it's like being judged side-by-side, day in day out against the best handpicked talent in the business.

In the chapters that follow we'll talk more about the behaviours that are expected of senior level executives and the characteristics that set them aside from the rest.

At this point, you're probably asking yourself – is this really for me?

Two of the key characteristics of successful senior leaders, particularly during this development stage of their career is that they possess higher levels of energy and the ability and clarity to focus this energy to achieve business and personal objectives.

They understand the importance of managing their ambition, and how to ensure that they are consistently exceeding expectations.

CHAPTER 6

PEER SUPPORT

THE IMPORTANCE OF PEER SUPPORT

One of the biggest shortcomings that differentiates managers from great leaders is inter-personal skills and empathy. Managers are often too busy 'managing' people to understand that team success and even personal development is not simply about what your colleagues think but also how they feel.

Of course, there are countless examples of ruthless yet successful CEOs who lack any real empathy for their employees or peers, but in an era of direct mass communication, not just with your staff but also your customers, being objectionable is a hard way to earn respect.

How you treat and interact with your peers can both risk alienating those close to you but also vindicate the views of your doubters. It is likely that your peers will play a part in you achieving your career objectives. Often they are asked to comment on their perception of you – they have both the power to support your cause or potentially destroy it!

For all the business acumen and performance results, being able to demonstrate an ability to bring creative ideas and constructive feedback to a table, while offering mentorship and guidance will do more to drive results and loyalty than most heavy-handed approaches. The power of leadership is to be able to not only communicate your organization's vision and objectives but to inspire passion and belief from those around you in what you want to achieve.

And in order, to achieve those results you need to take the right people with you on your journey.

That journey will rarely be either smooth or linear. As the saying goes 'no man is an island' and you will never know precisely where or when you'll meet those colleagues that can help you obtain your next career step or ultimately fulfil your ambition.

They may be the individuals who can connect you to the right role or introduce you to the right contact. They may be the person who speaks up about your talents and skills at the right moment in a meeting or the boss who decides to take you with them on their own career progression.

The simple fact is – we meet people every day, and every contact has the potential to change your career and life forever.

Whilst you may be an excellent judge of character and know an 'influencer' the moment you meet them, you're unlikely to control when, where or how you make these critical connections.

Therefore, it is key that you can identify and then communicate your key skills and attributes in an honest and unambiguous way.

Your self-perception and the way people are led to perceive you from the moment of first contact (be it your name in conversation, via a LinkedIn invite or a chance meeting at a networking event) must align.

Understanding the correlation between how you perceive yourself and how others perceive you is perhaps the single most important factor in your success or failure.

The differences in perception are even more apparent between the sexes. In 2011, the Institute of Leadership and Management (ILM), in the UK, surveyed British managers with men consistently overestimating their abilities and performance, while women underestimated; both despite their overall performances being judged to have not differed in quality. Over half of all female respondents reported self-doubt about both their day-to-day performance and their overall careers, compared to under a third of the men surveyed.

Simple things, such as your own belief that you are effective and assertive in how you communicate could vary from colleagues perceiving you to being abrupt and unsupportive, and at the opposite end of the spectrum another feeling you are weak and inadequate.

Recent research in the Personality and Social Psychology Bulletin entitled *'Pushing in the Dark: Causes and Consequences of Limited Self-Awareness for Interpersonal Effectiveness,'* revealed that over half the time, people were wrong about how others perceived them. Fifty seven percent of people who were judged to be under-assertive actually thought they came across as assertive, or even over-assertive while at the same, 56% of people who were seen as over-assertive thought they were suitably moderate or restrained.

This inability to gage how others perceive us has a number of negative consequences such as weaker negotiating and pitching skills, and lower quality interactions with customers and colleagues where you are unable to measure the balance of the relationship.

Employers are looking for a director or C-level executive who has earned the respect of their colleagues and peers and who can use those relationships to bring long-term value to the job role and bottom line. In particular, they are looking for evidence that:

- You can communicate the organizations values and objectives effectively and inspire colleagues to achieve these goals.
- You can collaborate effectively with colleagues and peers at all levels of the organization to reach win-win outcomes.
- You are effective at providing those you manage (and those you don't) with constructive feedback in a timely and effective manner.
- You always transact with balance, bringing maturity and emotional awareness to all interactions.
- You have an outstanding track record of delivering not just on bottom-line results but also wider organizational commitments.
- You treat people with respect.
- The people you lead see congruency between the vision you are communicating and your actions.

For those that fail to attain this level of expectation, there is a real risk of alienating individuals, especially when you come across as an individual who's self-belief (arrogance) and career ambitions exceed your ability.

WHY SELF-PERCEPTION REALLY MATTERS

"No one can discover you until you do. Exploit your talents, skills and strengths and make the world sit up and take notice." Rob Liano

Socrates's principle, *'know thyself'* has been a business imperative for centuries. Understanding how you perceive yourself is important because:

- A positive self-perception demonstrates a strong sense of identity and self-belief in your capabilities. Those demonstrating justifiable self-belief are more likely to add value to the business and to work to further develop their knowledge and skills. On the flipside, there is a fine line between self-confidence, arrogance and being delusional. It is unsurprising that many poor performers often have inflated opinions of their own abilities.
- A negative self-perception, on the other hand, is an indication that you are lacking in confidence and failing to connect with both your work or the value you add. This negativity and lack of self-belief is likely to stall your career but also create doubt in the mind of your colleagues. Whilst talent can shine through; you are 'your' most powerful ambassador.

For businesses, the most important thing when appointing new executives is to find individuals whose skill sets not only complement the existing team but also enhance that teams capabilities.

As serial entrepreneur, Guy Kawasaki famously said, "Good people hire people that are better than themselves."

But most aspiring individuals think of themselves as indispensable to the success of an organization – a belief that can have both negative and positive implications. It can:

- Influence your career choices, in so much as a positive perception means you are more likely to take on new challenges, while a negative frame of mind can be self-perpetuating and stunt ambition.
- Impact your perceived self-worth in terms of status, expectations and remuneration.
- Have a direct impact on others and how they perceive you. Self-confidence instils others with belief in you, whereas self-doubt may lead others to be less likely to take a chance on you.

The dynamic senior executive recognizes that the ultimate benchmark of success is whether they will leave a company in a better position than when they joined.

In order to track success, you need to measure progress – both in terms of the business and personal development.

The leadership imperative includes all facets of how you interact with the environment around you. Authenticity is key.

It is through our daily contact with customers, peers, subordinates, suppliers, competitors and even family and friends that perceptions are shaped.

It is a social construct and one that changes continually. Every action and intervention you make impacts upon the way you are currently perceived.

People who have known you the longest or are the closest to you use each interaction to build this evolving perception, but for new contacts, this first interaction will inextricably link how you are perceived from that moment forth. How could we forget 'first impressions count.'

The most successful executives are those that don't just inspire others but in the process of leading, they learn. They understand that working with teams, in growth businesses involves continually adapting and learning and they recognize that understanding their own complexities is part of becoming a better leader.

An experiment at Manchester Business School asked students about their estimated salary worth after graduation – the gulf between male and female candidates was noticeable. Men, on average believed that they were worth a salary of $80,000 or nearly 20% more than the $64,000 that women felt was fair.

In a 2003 study of female subjects Cornell and Washington State University psychologists explored the relationship between confidence and competence. The findings were; the less competent people, the more they overestimate their abilities.

Failing to balance your self-perception and how others perceive you can result in:

- A failure to engage staff in the vision and mission of the business. This is largely due to the differences in how you perceive you have communicated the objectives of the business versus what employees view as a lack of clarity and, therefore, buy-in to the organizations strategic plans.
- A gulf between what you say and your actions. Staff and customers will judge your performance not only on how you communicate the vision of the business but how you personally implement that strategy.

HOW TO WIN FRIENDS AND INFLUENCE PEOPLE IN THE WORKPLACE

"It isn't what you have or who you are or where you are or what you are doing that makes you happy or unhappy. It is what you think about it"
Dale Carnegie, *How to Win Friends and Influence People*

Self-awareness is imperative.

Acknowledging issues, a willingness to evaluate feedback and ability to analyze how the way you conduct yourself influences those around you, is all part of embracing your strengths and using others' perceptions to help you develop into a better leader.

Team buy-in is essential for the successful implementation of both your personal and the businesses goals. The ability to build strong professional relationships and assert a positive influence over those individuals, so that they support your objectives is critical to the success of projects you lead.

And there's a further reason strong and healthy relationships with colleagues are important to your career success; happiness.

Happiness is one of the most important competitive advantages in the modern economy. Research shows that being happy in what you do makes you 31% more productive, drives sales 37% higher and results in people perceiving you as being both more charismatic and more creative.

People who invest in building quality professional relationships often 'give' the most in terms of positive contribution, mentoring, advice and by assisting their colleagues – the further upside is that these individuals are 40% more likely to get a promotion than those who don't contribute.

In order to earn that buy-in, as a leader you need to continually demonstrate your integrity, honesty, readiness and reliability in all your interactions across the business.

The easiest way to damage the trust others have in your professional capabilities is by being unprepared.

Readiness not only relates to being organized and turning up well-briefed but also to never bringing up a problem without possessing an idea or solution about how to negate it. The boss, who is critical of his teams' performance, provides no constructive value unless he has a genuine and considered solution as to how they could have performed better.

The consistency and manner in which you engage and treat people will equally shape opinion. Much of what people think and remember about you has less to do with what you say as opposed to the way you make them feel. **People always remember how you made them feel.** Do you make a lasting first impression when you meet new colleagues?

Whilst your focus is on building relationships that help develop your career prospects, think also about what those around you get from their interactions with you – do they get the positive benefit and do they enjoy working with you?

When you interact with colleagues, do you:

- Show a genuine interest in what your team want to achieve in their careers? Do you understand the ambitions and objectives of those around you? Helping others reach their goals is an important part of influencing your peers to support your own career ambitions.
- Are you honest and transparent in the way you communicate? Relationships with your co-workers must be open and honest at all times. Ambiguity breeds uncertainty, and you cannot afford to have your team doubting your abilities.
- Foster team inclusion and recognize achievement? One way to tell if you're building a strong team is your ability to retain top talent – have any star employees left or started talking about leaving? Supporting the careers of others is a critical part of a leader's role.
- Show a consistent interest in your team's happiness? This means not just work, but things in life that are important to them? Do you know about their passions, interests or personal challenges in a way that is more than just a fleeting glance? Finding common-interests is a great way to build a rapport with team members on an individual one-to-one basis.
- Ensure you are approachable in times of personal or professional crisis? Every situation in life whether at home or in the office can manifest itself in a way that can negatively impact upon your colleague's

performance and happiness – do you foster relationships where colleagues feel they can rely on you for support?

- Show confidence when networking with more senior executives or C-level colleagues? Transacting with balance and being able to hold and sustain memorable interactions with senior colleagues is tough but remember that such mentoring relationships add value for all parties, the mentor, the organization and you.
- Do you spend enough time considering what it means to be likable? It's not just about buying the first round at the bar – being likable is about leaving colleagues with a lasting positive impression – do your current colleagues enjoy spending time with you? If not, they're unlikely to be fully supporting you.

Each individual's perception is different, and it is also their reality – regardless of how right or wrong you think they may be. No matter what opinion you have of yourself, your success as a leader will be constructed not just by your actions but by the people you work and interact with.

Leaders invest time in building and nurturing a relationship. They make time for people regardless of how busy their schedule is.

> A desire for promotion is not a time to explicitly go into competition with your peers as author Marshall Goldsmith states in his best-selling book: '*What Got You Here, Won't Get You There: How successful people become even more successful*', "One successful principle of those trying to gain senior promotion is not trying to win everything".

In the context of THRIVE 'winning' is creating synergy with those who have an influence on the way you are seen – that is very much your peers.

UNDERSTANDING WHAT YOUR BOSS REALLY THINKS ABOUT YOU

Relationships in work are like those in life, unique – not every employee will have the same relationship with every boss or senior colleague.

You, as a senior ambitious manager are relying on your boss to provide the opportunities to demonstrate your ability on a wider stage and to facilitate the introductions and connections to develop your career.

What every relationship does directly involve, is people – a minimum of two (but, in reality, it involves everyone who interacts with you both professionally and socially). The thing to remember is that the piece of the relationship that you have direct control over is 'you.'

Being likable is different from being liked – not every employee and boss will be best of friends so focus on being likable and held in high regard, as opposed to being overly concerned about being 'friends'.

Your responsibility in the 'relationship' is to understand your own strengths and weaknesses, and how to adapt to facilitate an optimum working environment.

Adapting is not about changing your personality but instead being aware of the areas of 'weakness', which particularly apply to your relationship with your superiors and to take the necessary steps to correct these.

A major part of being a boss is evaluating your staff's performance and potential – an assessment that is usually shared with other executives and HR professionals in the business.

In a smaller company, there are fewer places to hide – feedback is likely to be less formal, but more regular and direct to the CEO or senior leadership team.

So, do you have an idea of how they are representing you? Does he or she support your potential to advance in the company?

You need to understand how day-to-day your boss is evaluating you.

- Who among your peers is excelling in the eyes of your boss and what differs between what they and you are doing? Consider how your

work ethic, attitude, passion, teamwork, performance and results stack up compared to those around you – and what can be done to communicate your commitment or success.
- What does your boss say about you to senior executives or the wider organization? Is your boss conveying your 'pitch' in a way that highlights your performance and ambition? If not, then talk to them – offer up some 'sound bites' that build a compelling case for your credibility.

So, what is your boss looking for in you? Well, there's two ways to think of it – things your boss is looking for in you – and things you should be looking for in your team or future reports, if you step up to an executive level role. These attributes should include:

- Clear communication of your workflow and delivery schedule – are you on schedule, on budget and meeting all quality criteria? If not, your boss will expect to know at the earliest opportunity. They also expect you to prepared at every moment – all data up to date and on hand demonstrating you are in control.
- Effectively articulating the company objectives and communicating targets and performance. Do you demonstrate knowledge of key announcements across the business and upcoming projects, challenges and opportunities?
- Having an opinion and point of view on all aspects of the business, be it growth opportunities, current challenges, structures, efficiency, training. Failing to demonstrate an understanding and concern for the whole business can be construed as a lack of ambition.
- Understanding and supporting your team. As discussed in earlier chapters, senior executives are leaders who nurture and manage talented employees, as opposed to focusing on leading day-to-day projects. Your bosses job is to enable you to perform at your optimum – their focus is therefore on you as an individual, and they'll expect you to have the same knowledge and interest in the teams you manage. Are they performing? Are they happy at work and home? What is their personal ambition?

Ask yourself the following critical questions …

- Are you a leader or a follower? Do you win friends and influence people in a way that will help the business deliver on its objectives? Do you attract talented people around you and will they work for, and with you to help the business succeed?

- Do you deliver on what you say you will? From the smallest of commitments such as attending meetings on time, circulating notes or reference material afterwards right along the scale to delivering big projects on time – you will only be taken seriously if you deliver.
- Are you a solution as opposed to problems person? Do you manage difficult situations or make excuses? Leaders give direction, rather than criticise – they avoid attributing personal blame and instead provide guidance and constructive feedback – when projects hit difficulty they take personal responsibility and resolve it. If they cannot resolve the issue, they act with transparency and work with those who can fix things.
- Do you take personal responsibility for managing your own development? As we've said from the start – your career is your responsibility, no one else's – you alone can understand and articulate your ambition. You should be the first person to invest in your future and to demonstrate your ability to THRIVE.

So, how then do you work to build a strong bond with your manager? An obvious answer is to ensure that you have regular interactions with your boss, be it one-on-one meetings, performance reviews or team meetings. If you're not front of mind, you are not likely to be making an impact.

Importantly, never forget that just because you feel you are ready to make the next step up, that is not a reason to skip or avoid more menial or mandatory meetings or stop contributing to smaller projects. Every attendance is an opportunity to impress someone. **And you are always being watched!**

Feedback to your boss can come from anywhere, even the most junior of colleagues.

> Some talented executives we have worked with, switch on and off the quality of their contributions/interactions in meetings, especially if they feel they have evaluated the lack of seniority in the room! Remember, everyone has a voice, and they can use it to feedback.

It is also important to know what your bosses core areas of interest and focus are at any one time – what 'pet' projects is he or she taking a particular interest in and what KPIs are the Board setting that they are being judged against.

You should never guess about what matters most to senior colleagues, instead, ask them about projects they are currently working on, how it will impact on the organization and think about ways you can both assist in delivering but also how you can make them look good.

Every person regardless of whether they're a recent graduate or a senior executive has a personal interest in their career. Taking an interest in your bosses work not only demonstrates an awareness and willingness to support them but is also an excellent way to gain exposure to the types of functions that you are aiming to work on yourself. **Remember don't suck up to the boss!**

Most successful business people enjoy a bit of hard work if it's productive. But in today's connected world we are 'on' 24/7 and are increasingly short on time, with an ever-decreasing capacity to focus on the insignificant issues which consume a disproportionate amount of time. A major part of your job is, therefore, to help make your boss's job easier – to lighten their load by showing that projects under your control are being effectively managed.

Before taking on additional tasks, make sure you have the capacity and the ability to meet expectations – a risk of taking on too many additional tasks is that either you are seen to not have enough to do, or alternatively it simply becomes the norm, and you become distracted by work that is not yours.

Make sure then that when you're offering to take on additional tasks you have sufficient capacity and knowledge to deliver exceptional results and that you are setting realistic timescales, objectives and goals.

The last thing that any manager wants or likes is surprises – by delegating additional work to you, they are not only putting their name against the finished deliverables but also an endorsement that they believe you are up to the job. The worst failing any employee can make is not keeping their superiors informed of latest developments, or alternatively, they themselves not being in possession of critical information. Even appearing to not be in control can damage trust in your leadership abilities.

Additionally, when you are succeeding, make sure people know about it. Not every action or result requires a broadcast update to the entire organization but rather selected and strategically timed announcements.

The company newsletter or weekly team meeting are likely to be dominated by lots of such announcements so establish the two or three achievements which matter most with your senior colleagues and disseminate information in the most effective manner. Consider a weekly or monthly summary email reporting your achievements from the past period but also your objectives and actions for the next one and crucially – what success will look like.

It may sound simple, but you would be amazed how many people do not keep a record of their achievements or actions.

From the outset get to know your bosses communication style, both how they chose to communicate with their reports and how they wish to receive information from you.

Understand whether they are the type of individual who communicates directly what they want and expect or whether it is implied or inferred. Are they forward planners – do they expect to receive briefings on the day in question or a week in advance? Do they expect daily progress reports or a monthly summary – is this best done in a formal presentation, via email or in a one-to-one?

Learning how those around you communicate is one of the easiest early wins. It will set you off on the right footing.

Success in business is down to our ability to direct, guide and motivate those who work around us. Our skills in influencing, persuading, managing (both transactionally and transformationally), mentoring and inspiring those individuals are key in achieving positive performance and career progression.

Effective managers make time and take the effort to manage not only their subordinates but also their boss. They hold the key to conversations, which will shape your career – so investing in building a strong working relationship is time well spent.

Every relationship has different ways of working, so be open to new ways of thinking, even when they challenge your own views. Listen, absorb, analyze, digest and adapt.

CHAPTER 7
SEEK FEEDBACK

HOW TO SUCCESSFULLY SEEK AND UTILISE FEEDBACK

We spent time in Chapter 6 discussing how to build relationships and influence in the workplace with your direct reports, peers and boss.

In Chapter 7 we'll expand on the best ways of seeking formal and informal feedback; some of the key processes used by organizations and how to deploy your newfound understanding to better support your career objectives.

As discussed earlier, time and again; change is nothing new, it has always happened. The change, however, has become more aggressive, more transitional and transformational than ever before.

Without the benefit of a crystal ball, it is fair to say that we can all expect that this significant pace of change will only continue to accelerate as it is driven by new technologies, new ways of working and a more global working environment.

Organizations flourish where a broad and diverse range of needs, skills, interest and personalities collide. Diversity stimulates innovation, thoughtfulness and disruption – but it also can clash with culture, with language, with values and with ways of working.

The key, therefore, is to establish an environment where every employee regardless of their background feels they are working towards a common goal. And therein lays the importance and value of clear communication and feedback.

Alas, most employers and employees fail miserably when it comes to utilizing the value of feedback.

We live in an era where employee loyalty has reached rock bottom – gone are the days of a job for life. The millennial generation today build their loyalty to a brand or an employer based upon transparency, honesty and shared common values.

Organizations need to adapt to changing employee expectations in a world where millennials will change jobs more frequently and where the workforce will shift from full-time to freelance employees. In the US for instance, there are 53 million (34%) freelancers contributing an estimated $715 billion to the economy, while in the UK 1.4 million freelancers generate £21 billion and the figure is growing.

In large corporations, the management structure sets the tone – inductions and team leaders will instil the company values and HR structures that will govern your career reviews and feedback.

At the other end of the spectrum if you're in a small business or startup (which account for around 48% of UK and US private sector jobs) – you are less likely to have formal HR structures, but instead will be in closer direct contact with senior decision makers.

Regardless of the type of organization you work in, it is important to remember that feedback is as much about information sharing as it is evaluation. We talked in the last chapter about self-awareness and that by taking the opportunity to self-evaluate we are better able to understand our areas of strength and those for growth and development.

With technology enabling us to work in new ways, so organizations need to find new social technologies to engage and feedback to employees in a way that supports optimum productivity. We will see more businesses adopting cloud platforms to provide mobile access to team information and allow continuous assessment and feedback.

In a world where we are surrounded by information, feedback will become more accessible and visual.

Instant access to this data means that managers can now set more effective and fluid KPIs. Organizations such as Google are already using these indicators to measure not only performance against organizational targets but also against employee satisfaction – happiness and engagement – the tools that enable growth businesses to attract and retain top talent.

Formal annual reviews are going out of fashion as we enter the era of continual feedback and development.

Software giant Adobe decided to end all performance reviews in 2012, after discovering that there was a greater employee turnover immediately after the annual reviews – too often employees felt they were simply being labelled.

At this key juncture in your career, it is important to put in place the mechanisms that allow you to manage change – the ability to support those around you and, in turn, to be supported.

We are all largely in control of our own paths, but those that are most likely to succeed have developed strong support networks around them of friends, family and colleagues and they understand the importance of utilizing them.

In your current position you are already likely to be responsible for reviewing and developing a team of direct reports. The experience of reviewing and communicating feedback to your team is important in developing your own emotional intelligence and the openness to receive constructive feedback.

At this stage of your development, you should be asking for feedback on a regular basis. Use this to better understand how those around you perceive you, to develop your emotional awareness and to identify your key strengths and weaknesses.

Be careful not to over request feedback, for example after each presentation or meeting. In the eyes of a senior executive it could look like a lack of confidence or a need for reinforcement.

Focus as much on developing your strengths as resolving weaknesses – improving the areas at which you already THRIVE will provide as much, if not more value for your efforts than expending energy on unimportant factors where you are weaker.

Understand also that feedback comes from yourself and not just others. Continuous self-assessment and self-improvement is a skill worth mastering. After every project consider 'What went well?', 'Where did I personally add value?' and 'What can I improve upon next time?' but also critically recognise and reward yourself when you succeed.

Often in life it's not the congratulations or plaudits of others that means the most, it's the recognition you give yourself.

WHY GIVING FEEDBACK TO YOUR TEAM HAS A BIG IMPACT ON YOUR DEVELOPMENT

Change, particularly during times of economic uncertainty erodes trust between employees and employer. Businesses around the world are struggling to engage with the evolving 21st century workforce.

The Deloitte Global *Human Capital Trends* 2014 report (research conducted with 2,500 organizations, in 90 countries) found that only 17% of respondents feel they have a compelling and engaging employer brand.

One of the frustrations with this type of research is that it is too often only digested by HR departments and not used to constructively educate you, the manager.

The evidence is compelling. According to Gallup research only; 13% (30% in the US and 17% in the UK) of employees from 142 countries surveyed are actively engaged in the work they are doing. Just as worrying is that, '24% are actively disengaged,' indicating they are unhappy and unproductive at work and liable to spread negativity to co-workers."

The reasons, in part, for this lack of employee engagement are (according to a recent study by Accenture):

- 43% of employees feel they receive a lack of, or no recognition.
- 31% of employees don't like their boss.
- 31% said a lack of empowerment.
- 35% said internal organizational issues and work politics.

The key issue that jumps out from the Accenture research is a 'lack of recognition'. Processes which effectively manage recognition are also designed to support manager/employee relationships, workplace engagement and organizational support. The issues described above, whilst often attributable to a wide range of causes, can in part be managed as part of an engaging and effective feedback process.

And that feedback process is vital.

Feedback is about information. Providing transparent, constructive and effective feedback fills 'information gaps' which can have a negative impact on organizational moral.

The leadership development consultancy firm Zenger/Folkman published research in the Harvard Business Review showing that when asked: "Would they prefer praise/recognition or corrective feedback?" 57% preferred corrective feedback whilst only 43% preferred praise or recognition.

When respondents were asked about the type of feedback that was most useful to their careers, "72% said they thought their performance would improve if their managers would provide corrective feedback."

Ensuring the continued commitment and energy of your team is not only critical to the success of the business, to future succession planning (as we discussed in Chapter 4) but also highlights your own abilities as a manager and even your self-confidence.

Sounds obvious you would think, but you'd be amazed by how many managers either fail to recognise the achievements of their staff or simply feel uncomfortable giving positive praise.

Delivering impactful feedback is about timing and relevance. It's not about recognising everyday achievements – it's about recognising exceptional behaviours and achievements and intervening in a timely fashion when corrective feedback is required.

How you deliver that feedback really matters. In the Zenger/Folkman research, 92% of the respondents felt that, "negative (redirecting) feedback if delivered appropriately, is effective at improving performance."

The research goes further and concludes that individuals, "who find it difficult and stressful to deliver negative feedback were also significantly less willing to receive it themselves." The research concluded there was a strong link between an individuals' confidence and their ability and desire to receive corrective feedback.

Employees "who rated their managers as highly effective at providing them with honest, straightforward feedback [also] tended to score significantly higher on their own preference for receiving corrective feedback."

As an ambitious manager nurturing workplace engagement is critical to creating a sustainable growth business – it is a silent KPI on every executives job description.

Some key principles to providing impactful feedback should be:

- Whether providing positive recognition or corrective feedback it is important that feedback is delivered as soon as possible after the achievement or incident.
- Feedback should always be transparent. Of course, there is always scope for the 'feedback sandwich' of good and bad news but never muddy the waters with confusing or ambiguous communications or signals.
- Positive feedback must always be sincere – while negative feedback should always be delivered in a way that is genuinely intended to help the employee resolve the issue. Never give feedback unless you mean it.
- All feedback should be impactful and clearly related to achieved or desired outcomes. Failing to plan the feedback, focus and explain why an individual is being recognised or requires improvement will jeopardise future objectives and risks appearing unprofessional, reactionary or haphazard.
- You should always be consistent in the tone and method of delivery across your entire team. Never forget that employees will always talk and share experiences and feedback.

If you are sincere and clear in your messaging, your employees are far more likely to be appreciative of your interventions. Taking the time to consider, plan and explain feedback with them shows your commitment to their development and is a key way of earning their respect and support.

Younger employees, in particular, are not only accustomed to but also expecting direct feedback – failing to consistently provide this information will automatically damage their relationship with you and your business.

Conversely, if you are successful in your approach to feedback, then there is a clear link to increased productivity, quality of work, morale, accountability and development. A team consistently delivering on these performance behaviours reflects directly on your skills as a leader.

RECEIVING FEEDBACK – NEGATIVE AND POSITIVE

Effective leaders provide constructive or corrective feedback – weak managers provide negative feedback.

Unfortunately the skills of your boss are largely beyond your control, but the way you process the information is not. **You are always free to choose your response!**

Dealing with feedback of any sort requires a high degree of emotional intelligence and self-awareness.

Corrective feedback

This is the type of feedback which most ambitious employees find most valuable. Corrective feedback is normally a 'tweak' needed in relation to a behavioural or performance aspect.

As a success-minded employee, you must use constructive/corrective feedback as a way to show that you are willing to listen to discussions about your strengths and weakness and act to develop yourself.

As already discussed, 72% of employees say that such feedback helps maximise overall performance and long-term success. It also becomes an important point of contact and dialogue between yourself and senior colleagues as they track your progress and development against agreed objectives for improvement.

It also goes without saying that even if feedback is well intentioned and delivered in a positive and corrective manner; it doesn't mean that you will necessarily always agree with it and that it doesn't somehow 'hurt' to feel criticised.

Before we move on to discuss negative feedback, here are just some of the important steps you can take to manage corrective feedback:

- Take feedback in the spirit that it is intended, which whilst protecting the productivity of the business is also intended for your own professional benefit.
- Avoid introducing emotion into the discussion. Being criticised, even the smallest pieces of advice can hurt, especially if you're not

immediately aware there is or was an issue. Becoming emotional or defensive can often put people off providing feedback in future.

- Don't be afraid to ask for clarification and examples of areas of shortcoming but avoid debates and arguments.
- Use the feedback as an opportunity for reflection and to clarify objectives around your job role and future ambitions.
- Accept the feedback and thank your manager for taking the time to provide the feedback and agree on next steps. Your manager will rarely have time to provide a detailed written follow-up, so providing your own actions in a short summary email is a good way to both continue the conversation, demonstrate your willingness to accept advice and provides you with a trackable action plan.

Negative feedback

When the feedback is less about correction and more overtly negative, then it is your responsibility to make it positive.

Not all managers (let's be honest and say very few) are great at giving feedback. The danger, therefore, is that what should be simple corrective or constructive feedback, is delivered in such a way that it makes you feel personally criticised and can lead to resentment and a lack of engagement.

At this point, your relationship with your boss and your company will come under strain.

You have three options:

1. do nothing at all and appear ambivalent and disengaged;
2. act defensively and let the feedback erode your workplace happiness; or
3. thirdly to take it upon yourself to fix the situation.

Remember their perception is their reality!

In addition to the broad points above which remain relevant, here are some more specific behaviours and steps you should consider taking:

- Stay calm. A single piece of negative feedback from your manager is not a career killer, but how you react to that negativity can have a big impact on your future development. Becoming defensive or reacting with anger, tantrums or deciding to quit, may all release your short-term frustration, but they do nothing for your longer-term ambitions. **Most people who act this way end up apologising for their actions!**

- Avoid taking criticism of your work as an attack on you personally.
- Listen to the feedback and use the type of body language and tone of voice that encourages your manager to provide full, detailed and honest feedback.
- You may not always immediately understand or accept that criticism is due, but you must work to understand where the feedback has come from. Identify in particular the time scale, the individuals concerned and directly seek advice on how and what can be done to rectify the issue both immediately and in the longer-term.
- Good listeners, summarize and reflect upon what they are told, in a way that makes it clear to the manager providing the feedback that you really have been taking on board what they have said.
- Establish the immediate short-term action needed to repair any urgent issues before establishing the longer-term fixes.
- Clearly identify exactly what success looks like. This can be not just in terms of objectives and deliverables but also examples of colleagues whose results or behaviours best mirror your bosses expectations.
- Not all feedback is necessarily correct and like anything in life, it is both influenced by perception and access to information. If you find yourself in disagreement, then agree with your manager that you will follow up after the meeting with additional evidence to support your position.
- If you continue to disagree with the feedback provided, consider requesting additional training or perhaps mentoring opportunities within the business.
- Show people that you are able to listen to feedback, are open to change and able to take personal responsibility for your self-improvement and development.
- Initiate any actions as soon as possible, to show you both take them seriously and have the skill-sets to immediately deliver the required change.

Positive feedback

Positive feedback is great to receive, but it can also be embarrassing to some and have it's own pitfalls.

We've spoken at length about communicating your successes, yet at the same time, few things will risk alienating your peers more than continually basking in your own reflective glory.

How you handle positive feedback has more to do with your emotional intelligence, charisma and common sense than it does any hardened set of guides but as a start you should consider:

- When receiving direct praise, never make too big a deal of the success, with your skill and leadership the outcome was never in doubt.
- Look at ways to share the positivity by including all colleagues who were involved or supported the project.
- Communicate success in such a way as it feels like the whole business has achieved something and not just you personally.
- Use the opportunity to explore future projects or share key learnings with other departments and peers.

With feedback playing such an important role in our careers, our happiness and our success, it is vital that you understand how best to utilise feedback to develop and sustain your career ambitions.

It's important also to be aware of and tune into your emotions as you work and relate to others in the workplace. If the bulk of your work does not satisfy you, go back and do more self-reflection about what energizes and excites you.

You may need to revisit your values, why you do what you do and for whom. The people that excel and enjoy their lives spend their days doing what they believe is meaningful and fun.

HOW TO GET THE MOST OUT OF PERFORMANCE REVIEWS

The more senior you are, the less likely you are to receive direct formal feedback on your day-to-day performance. By now, it is expected that you already possess the skills to do your job well.

Instead, you are likely already to be in the position where you are increasingly managing a team of individuals and responsible for formal programs focussed on their development.

We've talked in detail in Chapter 5 about understanding and gaining access to the organizational talent agenda and performance reviews are an important step.

Too often senior managers question the value of performance reviews for themselves. This reluctance to engage or face constructive criticism can both undermine the process across the whole organization but also mean that such feedback comes as a nasty surprise when you do receive it.

Effective leaders realise that learning is a continual process – every aspect of a business from its products, customers, processes and people are continually listening and evolving and so must you.

The value of formalised annual reviews like the '360° personal performance review process' is that it assesses and benchmarks your performance and capabilities against the organizations leadership criteria.

Not only does it allow you to view and understand a range of feedback from across all levels of the organization but it also ensures that your colleagues take the time to fully consider the value you bring to the business.

The whole performance review process needs to work for you – it isn't simply something that happens once a year. There is no room for passengers in the process – if you want the right outcome you need to be driving it.

Not only have stakeholders in HR and your team taken the time to develop and consult on your review, but the resulting reports will be shared.

Your role in the review is to build a compelling evidence-based case that you are a consistently high performer, exceeding expectations and delivering additional value, not just in line with your current level of seniority but beyond it.

Your performance and results in your current role are the foundation for your push for promotion, but so too are highlighting your skills and behaviours (we'll talk more on this in Chapter 8) and how these reflect your future as a leader and not simply a manager.

Consider how you can best demonstrate that you are already performing at the next level and whether these strengths are apparent to senior stakeholders. Consider also the relationships that you have built; that will support your case for promotion.

While your performance is the foundation for the review process as you progress towards executive level, it becomes less about observed performance and more about results, gravitas and behaviours.

Have you demonstrated the ability to deliver effective and progressive strategies that are aligned with the mission and values of the business? Do you already provide additional value that can be linked to organizational innovation and growth?

Are you able to demonstrate the following key skills and behaviours (which we will cover in more detail in Chapter 8)?

- *Strategic Leadership*
    - o Do you help shape the strategic focus of the organization?
    - o Have you demonstrated consistent financial knowledge across the whole business?
    - o Do you effectively communicate and inspire colleagues to align with the businesses mission and values?

- *Results Orientated Leadership*
    - o Are you a results led leader?
    - o Does your track record demonstrate consistent delivery of projects?
    - o Have you demonstrated the ability to lead change?

- *Talent Leadership*
  - o Are you an effective communicator and listener?
  - o Do you influence and inspire your colleagues?
  - o Do you build effective and lasting relationships and collaboration across the whole business?
  - o Can you demonstrate that you have the ability to identify, develop and retain talent within your team?
  - o Are you trusted and respected by your peers and held in high regard across the organization?
  - o Do you demonstrate emotional intelligence?

To get the most from any review, start by revisiting any feedback or goals set during your last evaluation.

Consider which of your objectives are most important to your boss and understand what success looks like. Go one step further and think next about what your bosses career objectives are and how you can support them and add greater value to the business.

Leave nothing to chance and ensure you are always prepared to present your case at anytime – regardless of whether your formal review is 12 days or 12 months away. Therefore, keep track of the objectives above and document your performance. Prepare yourself for tough questions and for tough feedback.

How you react to positive or negative feedback says a lot about you as a leader, but also about the value you will take from a formal review process. If you struggle to engage with a formal review, you are likely to find the focus and intensity of the talent pool even harder to work in.

Leaders differentiate themselves from managers by using the feedback and data as a tool for self-improvement. It isn't something they simply wait for or accept – they seek out feedback and act upon it, building their skills and gravitas.

EMBRACING A BUSINESS MENTOR

Whether an SME owner, ambitious corporate climber or startup entrepreneur we all have individuals we aspire to be more like – it may be their business acumen, their achievements, their innovation or their lasting legacy that we look up to.

Broadly speaking, business mentors fall into one of three categories, which we will focus on in the next three sections:

- mentors;
- sponsors; and
- business coaches.

The nature and focus of each of these individuals are usually determined by your objectives. They are there to work with you on understanding feedback and championing your development and progression.

If you are looking to develop your career then your mentor, coach or sponsors are most likely to be selected upon their position of influence. If however, you are more focused on personal development then decisions of the right potential mentors should be made based upon the level of contact they can offer and chemistry they have with you.

Mentors, for the most part, are experienced colleagues who can act to support you, sharing advice and being on hand to discuss issues. The mentor/mentee relationship tends to be a largely one-way relationship of support for you as the aspiring candidate.

Sponsors, on the other hand, are more likely to be senior executives who have identified you as a highly talented individual in whom they place trust and expect results. This level of trust is likely to result in a far deeper and more lasting relationship.

Business coaches are often specifically selected external agents (although there are more companies recognizing the importance of having their own internal resource of quality coaches) who act as an enabler/adviser. They provide the opportunity for you to be challenged by others and where appropriate, provide accurate, robust and unbiased feedback/advice.

The 2008 Catalyst survey found that 83% of women and 76% of men say they've had at least one mentor at some point in their careers.

But perhaps surprisingly, most (67%) of employees found their mentors on their own, relying on their personal networks. Just 18% of women and 16% of men formed their mentoring relationships through a formal organizational program.

When it came to the seniority of the mentor, 78% of men said they were actively mentored by a CEO or another senior executive, compared with 69% of women. By 2010, 72% of the men surveyed and 65% of women stated that they had received one or more promotions within two years.

The lack of perceived success of some mentoring programs is telling, given that a 2010 World Economic Forum report on corporate practices in 20 countries, found that only 59% of the companies surveyed said they offer internally led mentoring and networking programs, and only 28% said they have women-specific programs.

When it comes to a potential mentor, broadly speaking they have the following attributes:

- They can sit at any level of the organizational structure but are usually senior to you and within the same job function – unless there is a specific skill or behavior that you are wanting to develop, in which case job specialism may not be that relevant.
- They are willing to share their skills, knowledge and expertise with you.
- They provide you with on-going feedback, emotional support, and general advice.
- They are an ambassador for the organization, highly respected within the organization and demonstrate positive skills and attitude and act as a positive role model.
- They take a personal interest in the mentoring relationship and work to develop your skills, behaviours, competence, engagement and sense of fulfilment.
- They place personal emphasis on the HR and leadership development function of the organization.

- They are effective at providing feedback to you and other influencers within the business.
- They have an ability to understand and focus on your personal and professional development needs.
- They are motivated and lead by example.

While mentors bring a lot of support to the table, ultimately they are only there to provide you with the tools to succeed – the hard work still rests on your shoulders.

SEEKING OUT THE RIGHT INTERNAL SPONSOR OR CHAMPION

We've discussed in detail in Chapter 6 about building relationships with peers, influencers and across different departments in the organization, but there are further relationships to build and nurture.

Many larger organizations have formalised mentoring programs for high-potential employees. At technology giant Dell, those in the talent pool work with managers to create a development plan to prepare them for future roles.

Ultimately, however, hard work and results are not enough in themselves – you need people within your organization to recognize your potential and help you develop.

This plan combines training, on-the-job experiences, cross-organizational project work and mentoring from peers and senior directors. The purpose is to develop networks in which employees can give and receive feedback – a process which is supported with external coaching to provide guidance and support to help individuals better perform and develop their leadership capabilities.

But successful candidates go one step further. They find sponsors and not just mentors.

The difference – mentors are there to provide support through giving you their time and advice. They are listeners.

You cannot ask someone to be your sponsor like you can a mentor.

Sponsors champion your cause. They are senior influencers within your organization and have the power to get you the promotion you want. They truly believe in your potential and are prepared to put their name to endorsing you.

A sponsor might be your boss or even your boss' boss.

A well-cited article from *Harvard Business Review* entitled 'Why Men Still Get More Promotions Than Women', highlights just some of the problems particularly women face:

"All mentoring is not created equal, we discovered. There is a special kind of relationship—called sponsorship—in which the mentor goes beyond giving feedback and advice and uses his or her influence with senior executives to advocate for the mentee. Our interviews and surveys alike suggest that high-potential women are over-mentored and under-sponsored relative to their male peers—and that they are not advancing in their organizations. Furthermore, without sponsorship, women not only are less likely than men to be appointed to top roles but may also be more reluctant to go for them."

Sponsors have five key attributes:

- They believe in your potential and are prepared to stake their own reputation on you delivering and, therefore, expect you to consistently exceed expectations.
- They only work with star performers who deliver an added value which compliments their own skills and knowledge.
- They are senior executives who have significant influence and are willing to champion your cause if you can demonstrate gravitas and that you are capable, trustworthy and loyal.
- They provide access to opportunities and risk taking but in return expect you to deliver exceptional results.
- They provide access to their network and grant exposure to career opportunities. Your failure to obtain a promotion will be viewed as much as their failure, as your own.

While mentors focus on listening and advising, sponsors are doers. A sponsorship relationship is a two-way win-win relationship – you gain access to knowledge and influence while the sponsor gains the services of the rising star of the organization.

Be warned. As with obtaining 360° feedback from senior executives, getting feedback from a sponsor carries an explicit expectation. On parting their lips it becomes an expectation that you will do. Failing to action is not an option!

Sponsors, therefore, make your success their business.

HOW A BUSINESS COACH HELPS PROVIDE FOCUS AND FEEDBACK

There is for some a common misconception that business coaching is 'remedial'. Fortunately, this perception is becoming dated!

A business coach should be less of a 'crisis councillor' and more like a personal trainer at the gym. Effective coaches, like trainers, aren't a short-term New Years resolution. Instead, they are on hand to map and support their clients and help them to develop and operate at the very top of their game.

Consider top athletes – when British tennis player Andy Murray appointed seven time Grand Slam Champion Ivan Lendl as his coach, he went from a perennial nearly to a US Open and then Wimbledon Champion within 12 months. The truth is that behind every successful athlete is an experienced, skilled and carefully selected coach that works with their client to develop long-term high performance and not just fix problems.

A successful business coach can be a game-changer. They should provide clarity, focus and feedback – help you look at challenges like never before, provide insight and feedback to guide your decisions and help you develop the sort of self-awareness that will help you THRIVE.

So why don't more business leaders take the same approach?

As a successful manager, you are already dealing with rapidly changing markets, technologies, workforces and increased financial and legal scrutiny. But when it comes to making big decisions, the buck currently doesn't stop with you – it stops with your manager or MD, the person at the top.

Taking a step towards promotion is also taking a step towards effectively managing additional pressures and expectations. Are you ready to go it alone?

In today's business environment the performance, expectations and professional standards of the executive are under constant scrutiny by everyone in the value chain.

The result is that in the past two decades, top executive failure rates have soared, with the Harvard Business Review finding that two out of five new CEOs fail in their first 18 months on the job.

What's that failure down to? Often it is because those at the very top of an organization, be it the CEO, MD or C-level colleagues don't have the right proactive approach to managing their own development, attempt to manage everything themselves and are more likely to take a one-sided view of issues; resulting in poor or slow decision-making.

These top executives are prone to suffer from stress and exhaustion while their businesses face risking lost opportunities and serious financial consequences. Staying focused can prove difficult with multiple responsibilities demanding your attention all the time.

This is ultimately why most senior executives lose momentum – the stark reality is that the careers of even the most talented and ambitious of executives will probably fizzle out. Few make it to CEO or boardroom level.

One of the most famous supporters of business coaching is Eric Schmidt (the former Chairman and CEO of Google) who when asked; "what was the best advice he had ever received," his reply; was "to get an executive business coach." Schmidt admits that at first he was somewhat offended and saw the suggestion as an inference he was doing something wrong.

Now not everyone can always afford an external coach and for smaller businesses in particular role of coach may be performed by trusted colleagues or your peers. Regardless of what size business you may be in, one of the things that always stands out to us is just how generous leaders are with their time, even when they have very little of it.

Great directors and executives understand the value of helping their best people thrive – they listen to them, support and challenge them, champion their achievements and earn loyalty and dedication.

The key to any great coach is that they provide perspective. A challenge for most successful executives and CEOs is the risk of becoming inward looking and blind spots developing. An effective coach providing an objective assessment is a reality check for executives.

Coaches do this by facilitating highly skilled conversations that apply a laser focus to an issue, (challenge or opportunity) that the coachee is facing. This enables the coachee to gain a greater sense of clarity, allowing them to decipher and examine their own options and with the coach's support, take action with a sense of motivation and commitment.

For some executives the experience can quite literally be life changing, for others it is merely a slight course correction, enabling them to solve a challenge or embrace an opportunity. For anyone being coached, however, they should experience an increase in their self-awareness and begin to unlock more of the hidden capacity and potential that all of us posses.

It is perhaps surprising then that research by Stanford University/The Miles Group of 200 CEOs, board directors, and other senior executives found that two-thirds of CEOs don't receive any outside advice on their leadership skills.

However, almost every single CEO in the survey said that they would be receptive to having a coach and that they enjoyed receiving leadership advice. Ask yourself; could a business coach be invaluable to you in pursuit of your promotion?

SECTION 3

BIG FIVE TIPS

1. Equally value your organization's talent agenda alongside the key senior relationships you have formed.
2. Be likeable. People will always remember how you made them feel.
3. Don't be selective as to when and if you 'perform'. You are being watched consistently, and everyone has a voice.
4. Be careful not to over request feedback from senior executives. This could be seen as a lack of confidence or a need for reinforcement
5. Be great at giving feedback to your team. This will enhance their performance and, in turn, your results – helping your case!

SECTION 4

LOOK AND ACT THE PART

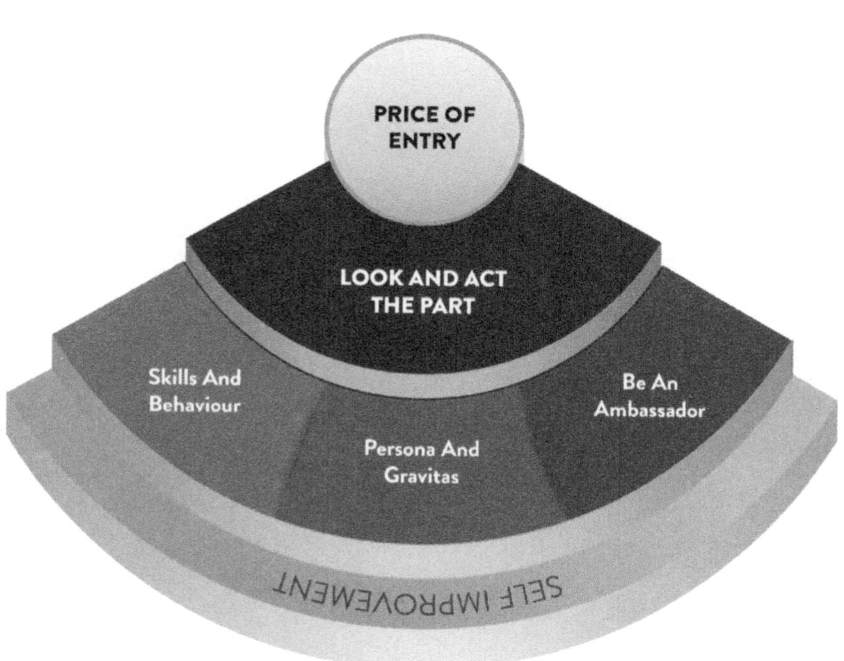

CHAPTER 8

SKILLS AND BEHAVIOUR

TAKING CONTROL OF YOUR DEVELOPMENT

Back in Chapter 5, we discussed the benefits of working with your HR department. But alongside engaging with your organizational talent agenda is the investment in terms of time, energy, resource and money that you make in yourself.

Whilst most medium and larger organizations invest significantly in people development – it's wrong to assume this is somehow your employers' responsibility.

Nor is personal development some sort of chore – going on a company course isn't a form of appeasement to HR, it's a small part of how you demonstrate your continued worth.

Remember most of us (recent graduates aside) have just lived through a seismic global shift – one that changed the job market forever. In record time jobs, companies and even entire industries disappeared.

The employees who failed to remain relevant in the job market paid the biggest price.

The reality is that most people are simply too busy working to stop and properly think about how to invest in their careers. Many presume that they are doing a good enough job and are suitably up to date with the latest training and developments – the truth is that you don't know what you don't know and ignorance, is no excuse.

Building sustainable success requires both self-awareness and the acceptance that you are the only one who can make it happen. That self-awareness requires you to understand the factors that will drive you to achieve your career objectives. You are accountable for your own success – no one else is!

Key to this is identifying your unique value proposition and how to both use and convey this. Successful careers are built on the skills and capabilities you bring to the business – you should expect to have to continually invest in those skills if you want to ensure that you retain a competitive edge over your peers.

If you don't add value, then no employer is going to remember you, let alone put you forward for the types of projects that are essential on the path to promotion.

Therefore, consider your career roadmap and calculate the ROI (return on investment) of the time, energy, money and sacrifice you need to make. The right sort of investment should be one that leads to not only self-improvement but, sustainable growth both in work and in life. So, make sure the choices you make align with what you are passionate about and your long-term career ambitions.

Investing in yourself and your career is a statement of intent – one that means your boss is far more likely to invest in you also.

Your personal investment requires an holistic approach to developing and refining all aspects of your professional persona – the 'brand' that you both live and communicate.

We talk about being yourself but better – about pushing your current boundaries.

But that also means you need to be smart with the time you have. Taking the steps towards promotion involves a commitment of your time – winning and then sustaining that promotion will involve a career-long commitment to continually exceed expectations.

Managing your career requires you to step out of your comfort zones. Very few people are confident public speakers or networkers – but your success will ultimately depend upon the impression you make, the authority with which you convey your brand and your ability.

Developing skills in speaking, communicating and networking are entirely within your control.

Focussed individuals, with a clear strategy for personal development will seize opportunities that come their way to make themselves more successful. Your success requires one important ingredient – a personal commitment to take personal responsibility for investing in and managing your career.

THE BEHAVIOURS AND SKILL-SETS OF LEADERS

When we started out writing THRIVE, we were conscious of our desire to provide a compelling but focused insight into the key areas all ambitious future executives should consider.

When it comes to the topic of leadership, there have been many (probably tens if not hundreds of thousands) books written providing in-depth analysis of the key skills and behaviours which successful executives possess.

We would do the subject of leadership (and you for that matter) no favours if we tried to cover that exhaustive research in THRIVE. But, it would be remiss of us not to touch very briefly on it specifically with regards to the behaviours that are expected of ambitious executives.

As discussed in Chapter 7, executive skills and behaviours cover three key themes:

- strategy;
- results; and
- talent (people)

1. Strategic leadership

Leaders help shape the strategic focus of the organization by:

- Developing and aligning their departmental priorities or functions with strategic objectives of the organization.
- Understanding future organizational needs and greater regional and global trends – they can articulate and communicate these across all levels of their team and the business.
- Delivering a data and insights-driven approach to decision-making that is aligned with the businesses wider strategic objectives.
- Effectively communicating the organizations vision and 'brand' externally.

Leaders demonstrate consistent financial awareness across the whole business by:

- Effectively communicating the key financial indicators with their teams and successfully managing budgets, financial performance and delivery within their department and teams.

- Using their knowledge of the organizational objectives, vision and financial indicators to identify and assess new revenue opportunities and mitigate potential risks.
- Understanding the businesses short and long term financial objectives and the financial implications of all decisions and expenditure taken.
- Understanding financial transparency and compliance protocol.

Leaders effectively communicate and inspire their teams and colleagues to align with the businesses mission and values by:

- Ensuring that organizations strategies and plans are integrated and aligned for success.
- Understanding positive and negative risk opportunities and the processes for managing and maximizing upside performance.
- Effectively communicating and inspiring direct reports, peers and colleagues in support of the businesses vision and mission.

2. Results orientated leadership

Leaders are led by results, they:

- Align resources and skills across the department to ensure maximised productivity from their teams.
- Accept projects that others may view as too difficult while at the same time not compromising the day-to-day performance of themselves or their team.
- Take a data-driven approach to delivery, ensuring that decisions are based upon sound documented reasoning.
- Understand upside and downside risk and take action to maximize benefits and mitigate against loss.

Leaders demonstrate consistent delivery of projects and day-to-day performance by:

- Balancing the achievement of short and long-term objectives. Holding themselves and their reports accountable for results and meeting deadlines and objectives.
- Ensuring all stakeholders are engaged and updated on the progress of projects.
- Being transparent and open when things go wrong to ensure no unexpected surprises.

- Taking responsibility and accountability for the success of the project and ensuring delivery of projects on time and on budget within the agreed parameters.

Leaders demonstrate the ability to lead change within their organization by:

- Fostering an environment of innovation where continuous questioning and experimentation with ideas both new and old is encouraged.
- Using all resources at their disposal including their people, technology and processes.
- Understanding organizational, regional and global complexity, trends and the impact they have on people, products and results.
- Creating an optimum balanced environment in which their team can achieve and THRIVE.

3. Talent (people) management

Leaders are both effective communicators and listeners, who:

- Can communicate and present ideas to internal and external stakeholders at all levels of the business.
- Listen to feedback from a wide variety of sources and digest and collate those views in order to gain a more complete understanding of their colleague's/stakeholders thoughts and opinions.
- Ensure that their direct reports have the appropriate tools, resources and information in order to deliver upon their objectives.

Leaders influence and inspire their colleagues by:

- Nurturing authentic shared-beliefs behind the business cause.
- Building an environment that enables both personal and professional development, in which all colleagues feel engaged and that they contribute to the shared success of the business.
- Establishing their credibility as a thought leader with a broad range of knowledge across the organization and industry.

Leaders build effective and lasting relationships and collaboration across the whole business by:

- Championing a culture of collaboration and teamwork across departments and teams.

- Building networks of internal and external influencers for the benefit of their team and the business.
- Investing time to get to understand people, their interests and aspirations (both personal and professional) and how the relationship can prove mutually beneficial.

Leaders demonstrate that they have the ability to identify, develop and retain talent within the teams they lead and wider business by:

- Acting as a brand ambassador who can effectively communicate the company values to internal and external talent.
- Working with HR and senior leaders to develop a team talent plan that identifies training and review processes to nurture talent.
- Building an environment where achievements are recognised and constructive feedback is used to develop potential.
- Identifying talented potential future leaders as part of a succession plan.

Leaders are trusted and respected by their peers and held in high regard across the organization by:

- Consistently showing respect for all their colleagues and interest in helping everyone in the business to succeed.
- Understanding and fostering diversity and individuality within their teams.
- Acting in a manner that is always transparent and clear – being reliable and honouring their commitments to others. Leading by example and displaying strong ethics and integrity.

Leaders demonstrate emotional intelligence by:

- Understanding their own strengths and weaknesses.
- Embracing feedback as part of their personal development and progression without feeling offended or criticized.
- Ensuring they work to their strengths while at the same time respecting differences in others.
- Being true to their personal beliefs and values.
- Practising 'inclusive' communication techniques to engage colleagues.
- Using every situation as an opportunity to learn and develop their thinking.

A fairly comprehensive inventory of executive leadership skills and behaviours for your digestion and we would suggest your assessment against!

While the core three themes are all important, often senior leaders will pay particular attention to the ability of an individual to demonstrate their strategic skill.

After all, it would be an expectation that you move into that space or at least step up.

It would be prudent for you to seek out any leadership competency framework (an inventory of skills and behaviours) that your organization is currently working to, as successful compliance with the framework is likely to be significant in assessing your readiness for senior promotion.

INVESTING IN YOUR QUALIFICATIONS

Most organizations big and small offer training as part of the incentive and personal development package. Embracing and engaging with your organizations development and training plan is fundamental to your professional skill progression in areas that are identified as critical – it's also as important in demonstrating your understanding of the importance of continual development and the belief in the HR departments agenda.

But it shouldn't stop there.

Most organizations expect talented individuals to go further than the training mapped out by the organization. Most HR departments will be more than receptive to working with individuals and their line managers to help identify additional training that can benefit you and the organization – that's an easy win and at no cost.

But many employers expect you to go even further. That is to **show your willingness to invest in yourself** – in your own success and demonstrate a commitment to being an exceptional and knowledgeable individual – not just in your standing in the organization but within the industry as a whole. Interestingly over the last 12 months, there has also been a rise in senior executives investing in coaching 'privately' – those self-funding.

So, what sort of qualifications do executives need? Is a degree or post-graduate study essential to your future success and if so where should you study?

Like most things the answer is dependent on a number of factors – but what experience tells us is that too many relevant qualifications are rarely a hindrance. Equally, if you've reached the point of pushing to pursue a senior level promotion, you've certainly earned experience over pure qualifications but now could be a great time to invest.

But it's a fact, Bill Gates and Richard Branson never finished university and look where that got them – right?

The key difference seems to be between those with the drive to found their own business and rising through the ranks. It's almost impossible to find a story of an entrepreneur thriving at college or university – the likes of Bill Gates, Michael Dell and Richard Branson are just a handful of hundreds of examples of business icons that didn't need a degree to succeed.

In fact, perhaps what is more surprising is the number of entrepreneurs who started degrees but soon decided it was not for them. JetBlue Airways founder David Neeleman dropped out of college midway through his degree, as did John Mackey of Whole Foods. And Matt Mullenweg started WordPress, which now runs 16% of internet websites, after dropping out of the University of Houston – in fact, it is something of a trend with big technology firms.

Daniel Ek co-founded Spotify at age 21 and lasted just eight weeks before dropping out of an engineering degree at the Royal Institute of Technology in Sweden. Mark Zuckerberg famously built Facebook into the world's largest social network having dropped out of Harvard University, while Arash Ferdowsi the co-founder of file-sharing service DropBox, dropped out of the Massachusetts Institute of Technology three years into his degree.

But the thing with all these brilliant business builders is that they did just that – they built corporations, rather than climbing the ladder.

According to the U.S. Bureau of Labor Statistics, "many top executives have a bachelor's or master's degree in business administration or in an area related to their field of work. Top executives in the public sector often have a degree in business administration, public administration, law, or the liberal arts. Top executives of large corporations often have a master of business administration (MBA). College presidents (or university vice-chancellors) typically have a doctoral degree in the field in which they originally taught or in education administration."

When it comes to the top job – in the UK, 90% of FTSE 250 CEOs attended university with the highest number studying economics and business (17%), followed by law and engineering – although more broadly over a quarter (26%) of CEOs studied arts subjects.

The Oxbridge institutions were the best represented, followed by the University of Manchester while eight percent of the FTSE 100 studied at Harvard in the US.

It's no surprise then that Harvard Business School leads the way when it comes to Fortune 100 CEOs in the US, over the years their alumni include the likes of Michael Bloomberg, Jamie Dimon of JP Morgan, Sheryl Sandberg of Facebook, Salman Khan, Henry Paulson, Mitt Romney and Jeffrey Immelt of General Electric.

So, having established that a degree level qualification is an expected given for many – but not exclusively a necessity…the biggest question is 'should an ambitious leader pursue an MBA?'

A Masters in Business Administration (MBA) trains you on all aspects of business: Finance, Accounting, Human Resources, Marketing, Sales, Operations, Strategic Planning and Leadership. Many leaders swear not only by the value of the teaching on an MBA program but also the life-long networks that are built by studying alongside fellow experienced senior business people.

Looking at recent statistics, in the UK 36 CEOs in the Fortune 100 earned MBAs. More broadly 92 per cent of 2012 business school graduates worldwide found employment within three months of graduation.

But deciding to leave the workforce and go back to school for an MBA should be a decision that you consider long and hard? If you're planning your roadmap to an executive level promotion can you really afford an 18 month to two-year break in your career? In this digital age, there are even on-line MBA options available – but they still demand a huge time commitment!

The reality is that an MBA won't help you become a superstar employee – but it can be a differentiator between you and another candidate.

The type of person who succeeds in being promoted to a C-Level executive role has an advanced skill-set which sets them apart from other employees.

But, yes of course, an MBA can help you develop those skills still further – things to consider are:

- Understand why you want to pursue an MBA. Are you doing so for the right reasons or do you simply want the MBA title next to your name?

- Is your current company supporting or encouraging you to study one or do you see this as part of a change in career paths?
- If you are planning to study an MBA you should only be looking at the top-tier business schools and programs of study that match with your career ambitions.

We've never yet come across an individual who didn't get a role because they didn't have an MBA – but conversely, if two candidates are sat side by side with equal credentials – to be able to demonstrate a commitment to a course of study at your own personal expense is a powerful statement of your belief in yourself. We have seen CEOs/MDs use this self-commitment/investment as a major differentiator in recruitment situations!

But, there are of course many, in fact thousands of alternatives. Most universities and business schools offer short courses, many by distance learning which may prove the perfect opportunity to make an initial investment in yourself without the whole-sale commitment of an MBA.

The other proven route is by joining a professional body – professional membership of an organization such as the Institute of Directors (IoD) in the UK makes a statement of your commitment to continual learning, whilst also enabling excellent networking opportunities. The IoD and most other professional bodies offer high quality short and longer term accredited training programs and a path towards higher membership levels.

In the US for instance top executives may complete a certification program through the Institute of Certified Professional Managers to earn the Certified Manager (CM) credential. To become a CM, candidates must meet education and experience requirements and pass three exams.

With so many options available it's advisable and beneficial to discuss options with your HR Partner – they're likely to be both supportive and a good guide in terms of how different qualifications or memberships can support your professional development. And most importantly, it further communicates your career ambition!

PERSONAL SUPPORT AND PERSONAL BEHAVIOURS

THRIVE is not intended to be a well-being book, there are hundreds of those out there, written by experts. But it would be unwise not to mention the importance of ensuring that you have not only a healthy work/life balance, but also a support network in place before you put yourself in the mentally and physically demanding position of targeting a senior level position.

As already discussed at length – timing is everything. If you're not 100% ready for a promotion, then you could risk doing lasting career damage.

Attempting to take on too much at once is a proven recipe for disaster – if your personal life is not in balance, then you will significantly reduce your ability to achieve and sustain excellence.

Whilst many younger managers have the freedom to pursue perceived riskier career moves, so major life events like marriage, a new house, children, a sudden grievance all have an impact to lower tolerance to risk.

As important as it is having professional support around you, so too is your personal support network.

It's not about being in a relationship or married – it is about stability and happiness.

Having your friends and family onboard could be critical in focussing you – ensuring obstacles outside of work are managed and that you time your push for promotion right.

Do your friends and family support this change? How will you handle any potential challenges that your promotion creates in your personal life?

Are they appreciative that you will undoubtedly be spending more time at work, under more pressure over a sustained period of time? There may be more time travelling, not just inter-city but abroad – are you and they prepared for that time apart?

Will they be on hand to provide a sounding board when things aren't going well, whilst not being a distraction when they do?

And are you sufficiently focussed on what you need to be doing in your personal life to aid your best performance at work? Whilst business people often talk about the long hours they work, there is plenty of research to suggest that balancing work and personal wellbeing makes you more productive and happier, so as you push for promotion you'll need the discipline to ensure you're focussed on the following:

1. Exercise is important for your body and mind. Regular exercise, starting at as little as seven minutes a day can have a real positive impact (and no, taking the stairs instead of the elevator at work doesn't count!)
2. A late night in the office doesn't mean you can cut back on sleep. We've all had to work all-nighters and yes there are times when you'll have to make compromises but you need to find your optimum sleep patterns and maximise your rest and recovery. Your success will be short-lived if you're physically and mentally running on empty.
3. Spend time with friends and family – something we all are getting worse at doing in the digital age, but well planned down-time with those who mean most to you has a critical role to play in being happy.
4. Get outdoors more. Never underestimate the power of some sunshine and fresh air, especially when combined with any or all of the other factors on this list. Taking breaks and forcing yourself to go for a walk at lunch time is an easy way to keep the mind clear and energised for the professional challenges ahead.
5. Regular activities such as hobbies, particularly ones you can share with loved ones, are proven to increase happiness. Likewise, volunteering and supporting good causes are proven ways to enjoy the double impact of doing good and having an activity to focus your mind on.

Success is about 'assessing the whole you'. Awareness of both professional and personal success orientated attributes will help ensure your transition into senior leadership and help make it sustainable!

NETWORKING – USING OLD TOOLS AND NEW ONES

Networking is a career-long commitment – the unfortunate thing is that very few of us make the time in our busy schedule to successfully maintain our relationships and networks.

Successful networking is critical to success, but it's not a focus of this book – therefore, we wanted to touch on some of the key strategies for using networking for career progression purposes as opposed to a lengthy deep-dive into the subject.

Very few of us really enjoy professional networking – not when the commitment can seem endless, and when it eats into our personal time. Nor, are many of us comfortable talking to strangers and being constantly 'switched on' to the professional needs of the business during conversation.

One of the secrets to successful networking is to build momentum.

The more people who you connect with means the more people who know who you are. As you develop those relationships the more they will come to know about your strengths and abilities and the value you bring to the organization.

Then the opportunity will at some point come to clearly state your career ambitions.

In amongst a busy schedule you need to make time to connect with the right people and create Grade 'A' Relationships:

- Identify those people in your network who are influential in your career development.
- Invest in building the right relationships with those individuals and invest the time and attention.

The more meaningful those relationships are, the more likely your name will be discussed in the conversations that matter to your career.

The benefits of consistent networking are that it:

- Builds your professional persona, getting you better known and letting other people know the work you are doing.
- Helps you perfect how you communicate your unique value proposition.
- Connects you with colleagues in different departments and will give you an understanding of how the whole organization works.
- Broadens your exposure in the wider industry – this can make you an asset to your organization.

Networking needs to take place both in person and online.

Social networks like LinkedIn or Twitter are powerful tools (as we'll discuss in a minute) but they are not a substitute for meaningful in-person relationships – so it's important to view social media as a way to amplify your voice and not simply a means of communicating from the comfort of your desk. No hiding!

An in-person engagement provides a human point of connection. It enables you to gage how people react to you and your discussion – the reaction to real-time conversation, body language and facial expressions are all valuable indicators of how you are engaging and performing in front of your audience.

For those who struggle to make an impression while networking, the following tips are a good starting point:

- We are all swamped with networking opportunities – so pick the ones with the best prospects of getting noticed. Before setting off, agree with yourself a 'timebox' – that is the minimum amount of time you'll stay and stick to it.
- If you struggle with confidence, then consider rather than diving straight into the middle of a group conversation – approach someone who is sitting by themselves and start a conversation – they're most likely in the same boat as you.
- Rehearse your introduction (your 'elevator pitch') and what you want to say about yourself over and over until you are clear and confident. Your name and job title are not enough – use an introduction as an opportunity to make a lasting impression.
- Positive impressions are lasting ones. So regardless of how bad the weather is, how much you don't agree with current government policy

and how flat the economy is, always focus on positive topics of conversation. And where ever possible rehearse your views with a sympathetic audience before unleashing them on the CEO or a senior influencer.

- Remember to ask questions which enable other people to talk about themselves. For example; how they got into their field of work or what their ideal customer looks like. This type of question not only forms a connection but also tells you something about how you can add value to the relationship.

Follow this golden rule; to be listened to you have to first listen; and to be interesting, you have to first be interested.

WHY IT'S IMPORTANT TO BE SEEN ONLINE

Digital is ubiquitous. It's around us and connected 24/7 – and it's the first place people go when they want to find out more about you.

Social media was once seen as a place for inane conversation, videos of funny pets and a way to keep an eye on the ex.

Now the most successful social influencers are those individuals who use networks to tell stories that engage a customer audience. They have an ability to distil information in order to build their own brand and online persona, position themselves as both authoritative in their fields and a go to for information and networking.

But it's not only critical for your personal brand; social media is now integral to the way that businesses, customers and employees collaborate and communicate.

The reality is that every day we are being researched and observed by potential customers and contacts we have never met or heard of before – and may never get the opportunity too, if we don't make first impressions count.

There's no denying there is risk involved with social media – it's in essence, a broadcast news/media channel open to the world. Social media has led to a blurring between professional and personal life, one where colleagues for instance become Facebook friends and where your private activities can quickly become public knowledge. But the risks of not being part of the conversation far outweigh the risks of a considered well-planned approach to using these channels to build a powerful voice that enables you to stay connected and relevant in an increasingly 'noisy' business world.

That's why 81% of employees believe that CEOs who are active and engaged on social media are better equipped to lead, and 78% of professionals would prefer to work for a company whose leadership team is active on social media.

Your line-manager and peers are also expecting you to already be utilising social tools to boost business performance:

- Nearly three-quarters (71%) of senior managers are using them at least once a week, compared to 49% of those in more junior roles.
- Three quarters of senior managers say social media will change the way that businesses operate in the future, that they have, where used, enabled them to be more productive and that businesses that embrace them will grow faster than those that don't.
- 59% of professionals in high-growth organizations are using social tools to improve business outcomes such as increasing sales and attracting and retaining clients.
- 81% of these 'dynamic' businesses that are using social tools report a significant impact on growth/expansion.
- 80% of high growth companies are using social tools to improve 'connectivity' (such as collaboration and knowledge sharing).
- 86% of frequent users have recently been promoted, and 72% say they are likely to be promoted, compared to 61% and 39% of non-users.
- Over a third (38%) of social media regulars are very satisfied with their jobs – compared to just 18% of non-users.
- 64% are very likely to recommend their workplace – compared to 42% of non-users.
- 43% of executives with socially active CEOs labelled their company's leader as inspiring compared to only 26% of the executives with CEOs not using social media.

And it's not just your colleagues that think that way, 82% of consumers say they are more likely to trust, and 77% say buy from a company, whose CEO and leadership team engage on social media. Take the Virgin Brand and Richard Branson (a prolific social media user) for example.

Being active online is a statement about how you view transparency and communication. The benefits of senior level participation in social media are:

- better communication (78%);
- improved brand image (78%);
- demonstrating company innovation (76%);
- it gives the company a human face or personality (75%)
- it helps the CEO build relationships with news media and journalists (75%);
- it has a positive impact on business results (70%);

- provides more transparency (64%); and
- it helps find and attract new customers (64%).

The key to building any successful online network is thinking from the outset about what your goals are. LinkedIn connects 215m professionals around the world, including 10 million in the UK but it's more than just a 21st century roller deck. Being authoritative online is about having your voice and expertise heard by those who have a direct role to play in your career progression.

Practice your approach, your message and know the right place to have the most meaningful conversations.

Building an audience and contacts on social media is about engaging an audience.

As a rule of thumb, we always advise that about 50% of what you say on social media should be conversational – this is most effective when you find online discussions where you can add and receive the most value.

A further 30% of your interaction should be about promoting content useful to your audience, such as sharing news articles or videos. There's no coincidence that many great business leaders are renowned for creating much of their own content, like writing thought leadership articles or blogs on subjects they are passionate and knowledgeable about.

The final 20%, is about selling yourself and your products and services. Keep this messaging subtle, targeted and unobtrusive to give yourself the best chance of generating leads and minimising the risk of alienating the rest of your audience.

If you participate in a dialogue on Twitter for example, be sure to follow it up with a personalized request to connect on LinkedIn and if geographic proximity allows, then use this as an opportunity to convert a connection into a valuable contact.

The most successful business leaders demonstrate the value they place on relationships – by engaging people in meaningful real-time two-way conversations.

The real skill is to seek to understand something about the individual you are trying to engage with. Use tools such as LinkedIn to research them and when first connecting, ask them not only about what they do but what they love about it or maybe even what they find challenging. Practice active listening – hearing is one thing, showing that you are hearing can be another!

Most important of all, your online persona should be interesting. Do the groundwork in terms of defining who you are and when you are asked 'what you do,' have a great punchy, concise, succinct and interesting response.

Your 'elevator pitch' or '30-second impact speech' is as important online as it is in person – the key is to deliver it in such a way that it naturally encourages follow-up questions…if you've nailed it the receiver will show further interest by asking additional questions and you've started a conversation with purpose.

CHAPTER 9

PERSONA AND GRAVITAS

BUSINESS IS ALL ABOUT SELLING

Do people listen to your every word, remember you and act on what you say?

If not, then now is the time to take action.

Career success starts with selling your personal brand. You need your peers and influencers to buy into and invest, in your persona, your expertise and your vision.

Personal brand building requires rigorous planning from concept to activation.

Are you able to think like your 'customers'? Can you successfully communicate with stakeholders at every level of the business?

It is the commitment to understanding and then delivering on their personal needs and expectations, that makes you both more personable, memorable, and investable.

Developing your personal brand is all part of your growth mind-set. It means understanding your strengths and weaknesses, learning and observing from those around you and becoming an expert in what you are good at.

Having confidence in your expertise and how you deliver that knowledge with authority is the fastest way to grow your gravitas.

From CEOs to military leaders, sports stars, politicians and entrepreneurs you will rarely find those who achieve superstar status in their fields, who have not successfully combined both personality and results.

This combination of the persona and result is what delivers the business '*X Factor*'. You must be able to stand shoulder to shoulder when dealing with senior executives.

When we explore the impact a successful company director makes we talk in terms of your persona and gravitas

Persona is the type of person and character of leader you want to present yourself as, namely:

- Are you moral and driven by unimpeachable ethics and values?
- Do you inspire those around you to trust you as a person and your judgment?
- Are you natural and showing the real you – false personas usually don't fool people for long?
- Have you built credibility with your audience through your words, actions and results?
- Do you conduct yourself with compassion and warmth that builds human connections?

Gravitas, on the other hand, speaks to the depth, substance and weight of your personality and presence:

- Do you know yourself, your ambition, objectives, strengths and weaknesses?
- Do you have a relationship of mutual-respect with your peers?
- Have you a voice at the key decision making tables – do your senior colleagues seek your guidance and expertise?
- When you speak do others listen and then act?
- Are you able to win over doubters with the strength of your expertise and your purpose and determination?
- Do you approach every situation with a clear sense of purpose but also with the ability to think nimbly and adapt?
- Because of the traits above, are you already consistently delivering exceptional results?

Great business leaders have an unmistakable aura. They exude a sense of confidence and control but not arrogance. They rise to the top of their field whilst keeping their feet firmly on the ground.

> Over-playing any strength can be a weakness. Over confidence can easily be seen as arrogance. It's about keeping your strengths in check.

The most successful business executives understand that gravitas comes from a balance of substance and style.

Whether it is Steve Jobs, Henry Ford or Richard Branson, each had an unmistakable personal brand that amplified their natural talents and made them stand out as leaders. You may not always agree with what it is they were saying, but you didn't doubt the wisdom, integrity and determination behind their words.

For those reasons, personal branding is no longer optional; it's a powerful and essential leadership enabler. It has also never been more relevant in the crowded and noisy world in which we are living – where digital media has given every business executive a voice and platform, regardless of the legitimacy of what they have to say.

We've talked in some length in earlier chapters about some of the key characteristics of leaders: in this chapter we want to explore the lessons we can learn on how they convey messages.

A confident leader inspires others to believe in their vision and commit to a course of action. It also helps to build and support the belief that those around you, have in you.

During times of change that confidence instils calm. Your gravitas and personal ambition must be balanced by your emotional intelligence and your ability to engage with your peers on a human level – with compassion, humour and focus.

Executive level leaders stand apart from managers because they don't simply pursue a job or promotion, rather their aim is to bring positive change to the organization around them.

That change takes the shape of both improved business results but also the lasting impact they have on the culture of the organization and on their employees.

We've already discussed that leaders are made and not born. While leadership presence comes more naturally for some, there are skills that everyone can work on; to help enhance the way you are seen, heard, and perceived.

Like anything in life, the more you understand and practice these skills, the more likely you are to succeed. Leaders with gravitas display many of these traits:

1. They understand that the best sellers are storytellers. The one thing that makes the likes of Steve Jobs and Bill Gates memorable is their ability as communicators to tell real human stories that relate to the needs of their customers. Whether delivering a conference speech, being interviewed by the media or writing in the company newsletter, great leaders are persuasive communicators. They define the organizations culture and mission and inspire and motivate their teams to follow that vision by talking with honesty, transparency, passion and persuasiveness.
2. They possess higher degrees of emotional intelligence and responsiveness, basing their decisions on a combination of data, experience and intuition. The ability to read people enables leaders to transact with balance when working with senior colleagues, and to get the most from employees for the benefit of both the individual and the business.
3. They are both determined to succeed, but also prepared to take responsibility and not just credit. One thing is for sure; great leaders don't give up regardless of the odds stacked against them – they get the job done by finding ways to resolve problems and overcome obstacles. They take responsibility for the performance of their team and not just for their own contribution and when praise is due they publically recognize everyone's contributions.
4. They understand the need to convey both realism and optimism through their words and conduct. Not only are leaders charged with inspiring their teams but also keeping feet firmly on the ground.
5. As discussed in Chapter 3, leaders develop an executive maturity that enables them to transact with balance. They are both self-aware and understand the intricacies of managing senior level relationships. They understand what is expected of them and approach every opportunity and challenge with composure and a sense of calm and authority.
6. Planning and preparation is key to building an authoritative persona, nowhere more so than when presenting. Great leaders take the time

and care to plan and prepare exceptional presentations by cutting through the noise to deliver concise and compelling messages to their audience. They hone their public speaking skills to deliver not just information but also a vision and story that keeps audiences captivated and engaged – striking the balance between vision and detail by presenting information in digestible sections and mediums for the audience to reflect and participate in.

7. They understand their own personal style that fits both their status personality and their brand. From a dress style that shows individuality and professionalism, to the tone of voice and choice of words and anecdotes, leaders leave nothing to chance. They know their audience will judge them, and they come prepared for that challenge, safe in the knowledge they are prepared and confident to handle any situation.

Leaders inspire their people to become followers.

Their knowledge, purpose and passion sell the company vision and mission and inspires others to believe in that course of action. That decision is based upon the integrity and consistency of following your words with actions.

Your gravitas should also go one step further – gravitas impresses people with more than just your words and ideas, it leaves a lasting positive impression of you.

By building this degree of admiration your people don't just listen, they act.

They have the confidence to speak openly and honestly with you, provide you with feedback and seek your input and guidance at the right moment.

THE IMPORTANCE OF PRESENCE AND BEING HEARD

Gravitas enables professionals to stand out from the crowd. They hold a presence in every room that earns the respect and attention of their peers.

It's not just in meetings or events, but in every aspect of their working day that an executive makes the time to listen and reflect on their words and actions. They use this presence to create a platform from which to share their ideas, experiences and results but, more importantly, to ensure people follow their vision.

Their gravitas can at times come from their role – the CEO or CFO of a business demands a certain degree of respect simply from their job title – but more tellingly great leaders earn the respect they hold through the power of their words and actions.

Strong leaders understand their purpose in any discussion and have the resources to adapt their message, presence and tone to fit their audience's needs.

(*Mindfulness in Schools 2012*) A survey of senior executives found 67% of the most senior business leaders saw gravitas as the key characteristic of an individuals' professional presence.

With 80 per cent of communication being non-verbal, senior leaders are adept at deploying their full range of inter-personal skills in any environment, not just in messaging but also in terms of personal attitude, mannerisms and appearance.

When we talk about leaders who hold a presence in a room we look in particular for the following seven traits;

1. The best communicators are assertive and articulate, using both their force of presence as well as words to hold the attention of the audience. Not only do they take the time to form and prepare their viewpoint but they also listen, and are ready to ask informed questions at the right moment.
2. Confidence comes from understanding the value of the contribution you make to a meeting, your team and the organization. Once you acknowledge that you have value to add, then that value remains regardless of who, no matter of how senior, is present.

3. Great speakers continually adapt and evolve their style – they improve their delivery and 'pitch' message by practicing their networking and conversational skills and most importantly by listening. As a result, they know what interests their audience and how to have their voice heard in any situation. They command attention through their presence, body language and a clear, concise and articulate delivery of ideas and insights, rather than through raising their voice or gimmicks.
4. Messages, spoken or written, are always more memorable when they are focused. Executives with gravitas, speak on subjects that they are knowledgeable about. Subjects where their insights add value. They ensure those messages are well researched, transparent, honest and clear. When preparing for any meeting, speech or event, they always ensure they know the audience and their expectations, while having the awareness to adapt their messaging if the situation requires.
5. First impressions are formed the moment you step foot in a room. Many professionals underestimate the science of movement – it is not simply about a lack of a smile, nervous twitch or folded arms. Understanding your own body language is one of the basics of building your executive presence – get it right and you can create an aura of calm and control around you. Consider for a moment the most inspiring TED talks that you've watched; great speakers own a stage, and hold an audiences attention, not just with their words and presentation, but with the way their presence fills the room. From the speed with which you enter the room, the chair you choose to sit at and the consistency of your voice – every aspect of your 'performance' will help shape the impact you make on your audience.
6. Passion, commitment and leadership all help create and drive energy behind a vision. Leaders speak with passion and optimism – very rarely does negativity help inspire a team. From your choice of words and messaging, to your tone of delivery and body language, inspiring your people and business to achieve success starts with your belief in the objective and is achieved by the way you communicate it.
7. Executives with gravitas not only hold your attention but reciprocate it in return by being totally 'present' and listening with interest when others speak. They in turn use what they heard to form questions and delve deeper into a topic. How often on the other-hand, do we see senior colleagues sharing their point of view but turning off immediately after they've spoken – replying to an email, scribbling a note or thoughts wandering? It's a real skill to give your 100% attention – one

that takes practice if you are to not only make the right impression, but also gain from the contribution of your colleagues.

As a business leader, being heard is sometimes tough, you're one voice at a table full of high achievers.

But the way to stand out is by combining your knowledge, presence and purpose.

Your executive presence establishes you as a leader and puts those around you at ease. After every key interaction, consider the value you have brought to the meeting and those present:

- Have you provided information or guidance of value?
- Have you listened and supported your colleagues, equally?
- Is there a clear sense of next steps?

Your emotional intelligence will help you understand and become more aware of how colleagues and peers feel in your presence and react to your ideas and messages.

PRACTICE ENHANCES YOUR CONTROL, COMPOSURE AND CONFIDENCE

Leadership means having the self-confidence to make the all-important and sometimes difficult decisions.

Every aspiring business professional wants to make a personal impact. You may be one of the lucky few, who have it naturally, but for most of us it is something we have to continually work on throughout our careers, regardless of past successes.

Leaders with gravitas have the ability to define a strong vision for the business and then deliver upon it. They build belief and passion for their strategy and robust arguments to support their position. Not everyone will subscribe to the vision, but leaders with gravitas are equipped with the knowledge and emotional intelligence to deliver change without alienating doubters.

As an ambitious manager within your business, you already will be used to carrying some degree of influence and confidence. As you push for career progression you need to use this influence to maximum advantage – but just how emotionally intelligent (EI) are you as a leader right now?

Take a moment to assess yourself, your current skills and application against the following seven key habits:

1. Do you know what you stand for and what you are trying to achieve?
2. Do you maximize your own strengths and show respect for differences with others?
3. Are you consistently true to yourself and follow your values and beliefs?
4. Do you make it your pursuit to make others great?
5. Are your colleagues inspired by your enthusiasm and passion?
6. Do you consistently practice 'inclusive' communication, whereby you talk to, and not at your audience?
7. Do you use everything as an opportunity to learn and challenge your current thinking?

Confidence is key. Self-doubt prevents you from taking the opportunities necessary to successfully lead your department or business.

In relation to confidence, digest and reflect on the following questions and statements. Where are you right now?

- Firstly and very importantly, do you really want to be a leader? Not everyone does, that's fine. But if you're not ready and don't have confidence in your ability then why should anyone else?
- Enjoying your work. Being comfortable with your work, role and colleagues is an important way of building your confidence. If you're not happy and having some degree of fun and satisfaction in your current role, then what makes you think things will improve with more pressure and expectation on your shoulders?
- Knowledge is power, and the most effective way to develop your confidence is to be the smartest and most well informed person in the room. Become a subject expert, understand the data, people, relationships and issues involved.
- Delivering exceptional results is not the same as seeking perfection. We live and work in an era when time is short and where results demand the best possible outcome rather than being consumed by the need to deliver the perfect result every time.
- Don't be crippled by a fear of failure. At various points in your career, you will make mistakes, you will face rejection, and you will face tough questions. Failure is a truth of putting yourself forward as a leader, so don't let fear become a self-fulfilling prophecy.
- Don't second-guess yourself. Once you make a decision, commit and go for it. If you never commit, all you will ever do is change course.
- Don't just say – do! Confidence comes from not just saying what you do but also following through and delivering.

Your organization wants leaders who display power, authority and influence. They want executives who are composed and who can handle uncertainty, change and conflict.

Few things can test a leaders composure and resolve, more than conflict.

It can shine a light on your strengths, and weaknesses, and open you up to scrutiny from above.

Conflict management is one of the most important aspects of business communication. No matter how much we all dislike conflict it is something that you will have to manage, and it will have a lasting impact on how you are perceived.

Effective planning, preparation and management of expectations all help to reduce conflict and tension.

Your emotional intelligence and connection with your people is then needed to ensure that you understand the inter-personal relationships within the team.

The best way to avoid conflicts within your team, whether professional, power struggles or personality issues, is through communication. Your persona and gravitas will have a direct impact on the way in which parties in a conflict position work to resolve their difference.

THE ART OF ARTICULATION AND 'BREVITY OF MESSAGE'

The words you choose say a lot about you as a person, your understanding of the audience and of the subject you're discussing. One of the greatest skills an effective leader has is the ability to absorb information and distil down until they reach the critical points.

When communicating, you need to understand the importance of both focusing on the point and brevity of message.

It's the ability to understand, motivate and inspire your team that will make you stand out from other talented colleagues in the organization.

Leaders take opportunities to say what they think. They have opinions and insights on key issues effecting the business and industry and share this knowledge with their audience. They also understand that they are the experts – not necessarily their audience.

Therefore consider whether these traits apply to you:

- Are you respected as an expert in your field and confident to talk to an audience big or small at any time?
- Does your confidence in your knowledge extend to your body language?
- Are you articulate and clear in your messaging?
- Does your thinking reflect a logical order that is easy for your audience to follow?

We discussed earlier about the importance of understanding your objective, topic and audience. Making an impact requires a message that is built for maximum impact. Here are nine quick and helpful pointers to follow:

1. Avoid jargon, slang or swear words and worst of all acronyms – nothing alienates an audience more than having to guess buzzwords.
2. Cut out bad habits including the use of filler words – increased self-awareness and practice will help you identify any words which you over use.
3. Use clear and concise English – remember that in a global organization your audience may not all be English first language speakers and regional accents can often lead to confusion.

4. Use positive words and phrases – but don't over do it.
5. Ask questions of people, listen intently and respond to their questions directly.
6. Use examples and references to real people and customers – familiar names are more likely to stimulate a response than obscure examples.
7. Never fake it for effect – fact is usually more interesting than fiction and whilst your opinion can be challenged, the factuality of it cannot be disputed.
8. Actions need to match words.
9. Be comfortable to ask questions of you audience (one question at a time) and to listen with interest and respond directly.

The less confident a person, the more they tend to talk – they over compensate for their insecurities.

In one of my most recent coaching sessions, I was helping someone tackle their anxiety before preparing to make an important presentation. My advice was to focus on the first 60 seconds of the presentation. Nail it! Start well and the momentum carries you. If a sports professional starts a game well, they are likely to build confidence and go on to have a great game.

If it helps, focus on the rule of three. Decide on your three key areas/points to deliver. Then use your physicality to demonstrate and engage your audience around those points. For example, use your fingers to demonstrate progress against the three points.

Over communicating, either because of nerves or a desire to make a positive impact, can not only lead important conversations off course and sound under-rehearsed, but they also prevent your audience or colleagues from participating in the discussion.

Consider these three important factors when deciding what and when to contribute to a discussion:

- Keep your message succinct by knowing exactly what you want to contribute and having the discipline to stop. Keep your comments as short as possible, clear, and on topic. Avoid restating other people's ideas or ones you've made previously – although quick summaries of what has just been said can be powerful.

- Timing is everything. Don't start speaking until everyone else has finished having their say and avoid the compulsion to rush through your comments. A steady and consistent pace of delivery and tone demonstrates confidence.
- Silence, used correctly, can be just as powerful as words. Understanding the dynamic of conversation will help you identify the right moments for pause and reflection. It allows a chance for participants to think, reflect and challenge with questions.

The words you choose to use say a lot about you as a leader and manager. We're not all born with the gift of confidence in front of an audience, so consider finding a business 'hero' who you look up to and study how they deliver their message.

Identify the behaviours and style that work for you and then practice and rehearse your messaging until you're confident of delivering it, in front of any one, any time.

CHAPTER 10

BE AN AMBASSADOR

WHY EVERY BUSINESS NEEDS AMBASSADORS, AND WHY THAT SHOULD BE YOU

Successful businesses aren't just looking for individuals who get results and make things happen; they are looking for those unique people who bring real added value.

Being a successful leader involves being an ambassador for the company day in and day out – internally and externally.

But far too few managers conceptualize and then embrace the importance of being a brand ambassador. When you consider the full implications of what this role entails it fundamentally alters the way you think and talk about yourself.

In today's digital world, brand equity doesn't simply reside within the business, but instead within the people who make the company what it is.

Businesses are not just about products or services.

Rather it is a combination of your product, your people, your brand values and the customer experience you deliver which are central to building customer loyalty and driving repeat sales.

Businesses are therefore increasingly reliant upon brand ambassadors – individuals who can be either customer's who promote the brand but also influential employees who can communicate and evangelize what it is that makes your business unique.

Just because you're not a CEO yet doesn't mean you cannot be a brand ambassador – in fact many senior leaders simply don't speak with the breadth of knowledge and passion necessary to sell their brand. How often have you seen your CFO or Head of HR out on the 'shop floor' talking to customers or clients – selling your product and brand?

Employee ambassadors not only embody what the brand stands for, but they also have the personal credibility and mouthpiece (such as being active on social media) to promote and provide visibility to your brand.

Forward-thinking organizations are moving to recruit active brand influencers and empower existing ones to better engage their audience online. And it's not just about selling more.

Ambassadors act as company spokespeople, they educate customers about products and services, they increase brand reach and they provide a timely support service.

e-Commerce giant Zappos is just one of many start-ups and corporates embracing the power of their brand presence on social media via their employees. By placing their employees at the front end of customer engagement, they are empowering staff with a shared responsibility for the success of the business as well as creating a more direct relationship with customers. In the process staff are encouraged to have fun which apart from making work a more enjoyable place to be, also builds brand image, word-of-mouth marketing and acts as a driver for innovation and product/user experience (UX) feedback.

Of course not all organizations are as forward thinking – but the principle of brand ambassadors is neither difficult to champion nor to adopt as a guide, regardless of whether your current employer recognizes the need.

And it's not just about 'new media' and online presence – every organization big or small is looking for employees with gravitas who can build conversations and 'buzz'. From writing for the company blog, to contributing to press interviews, to attending or speaking at external events, businesses are looking for employees to spread the word.

The key traits which HR professionals are looking for in a brand ambassador are usually:

- Do you have gravitas? Do your credentials and profile give you credibility to represent the brand and are you confident at conversing in the medium and at the level required?
- Do you embody the company's brand values? Do you understand the vision, mission and values and can you clearly and concisely articulate these?
- Do you have an existing network you can bring to the table? Are you already active at networking events in the industry, a regular contributor to thought leadership publications or an avid social media user who can reach out to customers?
- Do you have the necessary skill-sets? Are you tech savvy, possess good written language skills and are you clear and calm in crisis situations?

Whether they recognize it or not, every organization needs brand ambassadors and the skillsets required of those individuals run parallel with those of a top senior executive. Regardless of your function within the organization, if you cannot sell the product or lack the confidence and knowledge to speak to customers about it then you probably are neither interested enough in the business nor qualified to be a brand ambassador.

PROMOTING YOUR EMPLOYER BRAND INTERNALLY CAN HELP YOUR CAREER

Not only does your brand need to mean something to your customers but arguably, more importantly it needs to mean something to your employees.

If your business does not ignite a fire of passion and excitement in your staff, then it is just another job to them.

Creating a workplace where people feel empowered and impassioned about what they do is the most effective way to build a high growth business.

The 2012 Edelman Trust Barometer found that your average company employee has twice the levels of trust amongst the public compared to executives. And, never forget that customers are 77% more likely to buy products when an individual they trust recommends them.

It is easy to understand why – if your staff aren't excited by your brand, why should a customer be. The opportunity for you as an ambitious leader is to not only effectively communicate your organization's values and objectives to staff, but to make them passionately believe in the jobs they are doing and the company they are working for.

Not only does this sense of empowerment and job satisfaction lead to happier staff and customers but it also has a direct impact on the bottom line of the business.

How big an impact? Well, research by Gallup shows that those businesses with the highest levels of staff engagement saw share earnings up to 3.9 times higher than their competitors.

But as mentioned in Chapter 7, only 13% of employees are engaged in their jobs. There is a huge opportunity to push your people skills – the ambitious leader who can build and engage a team, creates a workplace where people are happy and believe in the vision and values of the business and product, and in turn will stand the greatest chance of driving bottom line growth.

Before you rush off to re-write the employee handbook and evangelize your business, remember that sound management starts small and with your own team. If the people who report to you don't believe in what the business or they are doing, then you will lack the credibility to drive change in the business – regardless of your passion.

Empowering and engaging your people starts-and-ends with communication – and you'd be shocked at how poor most organizations (regardless of size) are at communicating even the simplest messages.

When communicating the businesses brand values and educating your teams, you need to create two-way channels of communication. If you have a superstar team in the making (and we're assuming you wouldn't recruit or retain staff who weren't exceptional), then they want to be heard, they have ideas they want to share, and they want to feel as though they are contributing to the success of the business.

When we talk about brand ambassadors what we are actually referring to is free marketing powered by your staff. There's no surprise then that marketing teams play a key role in developing the story of your brand and showing your staff how to tell that story effectively – remember that the best sellers are storytellers.

Just some of the organizational and team benefits that we'd associate with brand ambassadors include:

- An increased internal and external awareness of the brand as a result of more knowledgeable and passionate advocates talking about your brand, answering customer's questions and driving engagement.
- An improved digital presence (including content) and organic search engine optimization (SEO) performance as a result of more conversations and sharing of information and links.
- A better customer service and UX service where customers have a point of contact when they have questions.
- A higher brand profile that makes it easier to attract and retain top talent.
- Linked to all of the above is a more engaged customer who in turn will translate into increased sales, loyalty and lifetime value.
- A more engaged workforce equals a happier and more productive team.

So, how do you grow internal brand ambassadors?

Start by identifying if the values of your staff match those of your business – do they live your brand and product/service values and what are their strengths? Have you created a positive work environment where positive energy abounds and where your team want to learn, develop and be challenged?

To lay the foundations consider the following steps:

- Encourage more staff to participate in other areas of the business such as marketing, product, customer support and sales.
- Consider how being a brand ambassador could help your team build their personal brand and develop their careers – in the process building your support network. Can you make it win-win?
- Provide them with the tools and training to make it as easy as possible to share the brands values, ethos and products/services. This could be enabling staff to use their own social media accounts, letting them hand out free promotional materials.
- Ensure their skill sets are tested – writing and communicating on social media, particularly when not all feedback is positive is a challenge which even the most seasoned of brand advocates can find difficult.
- Ensure that internal communication channels from all departments provide brand ambassadors with real-time information, knowledge and feedback.
- Teach your staff the power of connecting, building and growing their professional network and community around the product.

Consider the art of promoting internal brand awareness as a project. If done correctly, it can enhance every aspect of your career ambitions. It demonstrates your understanding of the brand; your ability to work with teams across the business and to communicate the brands values to your team.

In the process you are building your profile, helping your team develop theirs, all while growing customer engagement and brand awareness. The result is employees who feel a greater sense of being part of the business and it's success.

THOUGHT LEADERSHIP IS REINVENTING YOUR PROFILE IN THE BUSINESS

Becoming a company ambassador, brand ambassador or 'thought leader' is an excellent and often untapped way of telling the business how you benefit their bottom line.

What exactly is thought leadership you might ask?

Thought Leadership is about becoming an authority on topics relevant to your business and its customers – it's about answering the big questions in a way that differentiates your organization from its competitors.

How does it work? Simple. A confident, knowledgeable spokesperson is vital to any business wanting to build their profile and reputation – yet every organization struggles to find them.

It's not only for the most senior of executives – as discussed; credibility comes from your knowledge, not your position in the company hierarchy. The knowledge with the most value comes from the people starting and leading conversations that lead to new ways of working and growth.

Are you able to stand up in front of an audience of your peers and talk with knowledge, confidence and clarity about key industry trends or opportunities? If so then consider the impact and exposure which being an organizational spokesperson can bring.

People are more likely to buy from people as opposed to faceless organizations – for that reason advocate and peer marketing is fast becoming the most trusted form of sales.

Where do you start?

Does your organization have an active public relations strategy? Does it publish white papers or reports? Does it have a company blog? Does it run an induction program for new employees? Does it provide speakers or attendees for external conferences or events?

At a time when you are building your brand both internally and externally thought-leadership demonstrates the breadth of your knowledge, your unique perspective on big issues and creates credibility and visibility.

It will also give you access to a range of important influencers and departments within the organization. As such, it is important to work within the processes for such activity and never go off on your own talking to journalists or external bodies.

Thought leadership programs usually have a key sponsor but responsibility sits across external communications, public relations, human resources and brand and commercial marketing departments. This represents an excellent opportunity to win friends and influence people across the business – but a challenge to identify who you should be speaking to.

Six tips to consider when starting off as a thought leader are:

1. Ask your PR/Marketing team about opportunities to contribute to the company blog, white paper reports or press relations.
2. Create active and compelling social media profiles, starting with LinkedIn, Twitter and about.me and remember to manage your online presence with regular valuable contributions.
3. Speak with your companies marketing or social media manager and understand the company policy on employees participating in online conversations and how you can participate and help add value.
4. Identify a subject area you are credible in and start blogging on LinkedIn – once a month is a good frequency to start with.
5. You won't always have the capacity to write as much as perhaps you would like to, therefore sharing industry news and blogs from other writers will give you a volume of content without taking too much of your time.
6. When you start getting traction with your writing, consider approaching publications in your industry to be a contributor.

Once you've decided that this is the right strategy for you, then you need to consider how to action and deliver it.

How should you start planning your thought leadership presence?

- Establish what subject matter you are most qualified and passionate to speak about and the type of information and insight you would provide and why this will be of value to your peers.

- Consider who your target audience are and their needs and interests. Using your existing audience is a good way to start to amplify your message.
- Draft a conversation calendar for the next three to six months, setting out key industry events and diary dates/announcements that could impact upon the content of your discussions. Remember the most powerful content is the most topical and relevant.
- Draw up a list of the type of publishers and journalists who are relevant to your target audience and who may need comments and insights.
- If posting on social media consider paid media requirements to reach an extended audience and amplify your message.
- Use your conversation calendar work with your marketing team to find opportunities to speak at internal and external events.

As your profile and reach grows so does your company brand by association. Like with any form of marketing the benefits are many and varied; but ultimately what you write needs to solve a problem for your audience and those searching for answers on that topic – if those are existing or potential customers or stakeholders then you are bringing exponential value to the business. So why shouldn't they support you and shout about your achievements.

HOW TO BE MEMORABLE

Every day you come into contact and interact with colleagues and stakeholders at all levels of the business (and customers too) as well as connecting with individuals for the very first time.

The impression you make during each of those interactions plays an important role in your success – in part, this success is down to how memorable you are.

In a world where most people fall into the mediocre middle ground, being beige proves a significant barrier to growth. Every interaction is an opportunity to make an impact but it is also an opportunity to stand out from the crowd.

You want to be memorable for two reasons, your personality and your ability. Not only do memorable people make an impact but they also leave you in no doubt that they are very good at what they do.

Consider this as an important part of how you market yourself and one that you must continually evolve and refine.

We've talked previously about your personal brand and being memorable as part of that individuality and the unique added value that you bring to the business.

In a workplace environment we have opportunities everyday to make an impact, be it your ideas or contribution in meetings, your results or even the support you give colleagues.

There are a number of rules to follow to ensure that you are consistently making a lasting impression. Consider the following priorities:

- Always lead by example and ensure that your actions and words mirror your values and that you do as you say you are going to.
- Business leaders and entrepreneurs are more often than not, very generous with their time. And not just for the big occasion – they take time out of their schedule every day to listen to colleagues and ask questions. Demonstrating your willingness to be part of the team by assisting a colleague with a smaller issue can leave a lasting impact.

- Never be afraid to stand up for what you believe in. Whilst relentlessly arguing a point can be detrimental, never feel that you must back down if your conscience says it is wrong to do so. Be transparent and clear about your position and try to bring people around to your way of thinking – avoid dictating solutions.
- Go beyond the norm and add exceptional value to the business every day.
- High performers translate their success into happiness. Positive energy and body language reminds everyone that you are confident and fulfilled by your role and performance.
- Great business executives are first and foremost good listeners. When you are receiving support, information or insights from colleagues, focus on listening to what they have to say, before offering your opinion and contribution in return.
- Always have an opinion with substance and meaning that demonstrates your breadth of knowledge but also passion and interest in the subject matter.
- Always arrive at meetings fully prepared and follow up post-meeting in a timely and succinct fashion.
- Develop your skills and style for engaging a whole room – simply engaging or directing your conversation at one or two people risks isolating everyone else in attendance.

Throughout your career as a leader, you will encounter many situations where putting your best foot forward becomes vital such as when meeting with new colleagues, engaging with a client for the first time, attending networking events and above all meeting with senior C-level colleagues for the first time.

All these interactions provide an opportunity to make a lasting first impression and to make the most of these here are a few simple steps to follow:

- Conduct yourself with a gravitas and persona that leaves people in no doubt that you are already performing and transacting at a higher level. Body language conveys gravitas through your physical presence such as eye contact, posture, and tone of voice.
- Show a genuine interest in people, their lives (personal and professional) and their opinions. Understanding more about an individual

and what is important to them will provide valuable insights into their perspectives.

- Understand the importance of balancing, listening and speaking. Whilst your most valuable contributions will be from what you say, don't forget the importance of listening and absorbing what other people have to say. For this critical time, remove all distractions and temptations from the equation and show genuine interest in them – using what they've told you in follow up questions is a great way to demonstrate you've been listening.
- Remember the importance of being authentic and use it as a chance for your individuality to shine through by personalizing the conversation. Pay particular attention to using natural language.

Consider also that not all first introductions are in person. In fact in today's technology centric world many are online through social media, email and even webinar or Skype calls, so be prepared to make those connections memorable.

One of the ways to do so is to develop a personal introduction toolkit which can include amongst other things; a 30 word short-form bio which can be used on social media profiles, a professional bio image for use online, a memorable 'elevator pitch' and perhaps a memorable story that says something standout about you.

All these assets help paint a picture of who you are, how you want to be viewed and help you control and enrich the conversations, which you hold.

YOUR 'ELEVATOR PITCH'

We touch briefly in the last section on your 'elevator pitch,' which has for decades been one of the most important parts of personal branding but which you'd be amazed at how often it fails to make the impact you'd hope for.

In brief, your 'elevator pitch' is a short and simple introduction to yourself focusing on your position, a background to the business, an overview of what you do, how you add value to that business and what your aims and objectives are for the immediate interaction, i.e. if you're at a networking event then why are you there, if it's a meeting then what are you hoping to achieve.

Consider all the applications for a well-rehearsed pitch and how it gives context to your presence – as an interviewer or interviewee for a job (see Chapter 11 for more details), meeting a new colleague, sitting on a panel discussion, your social media profiles, talking to a journalist, presenting to a potential client or just introducing yourself to someone at a networking event – the list of applications for a good elevator pitch are endless.

The elevator pitch is a vital part of your armoury but like anything it needs both preparation and practice so as to help you avoid talking too much or focusing on issues which are not relevant at that stage of the conversation.

When it comes to developing your 'pitch', there are some simple rules to follow – the great thing being that for a little bit of energy, the output and application for a well-defined pitch are numerous.

Consider writing it down. As mentioned, writing it down lets you use your pitch as a biography on your online profiles such as LinkedIn or your company website – it's also the foundation for a cover letter if you are applying for jobs.

As a rule of thumb, while some experts suggest anywhere up to two minutes for your pitch, our advice is that short and sweet makes a greater impact and that around 40–60 seconds should be sufficient. By that account your written pitch should be around two-thirds of an A4 sheet of typed copy or around 150–200 words.

The formulae that we subscribe to, is introduce yourself by first name (if in an informal environment) or full name (if more formal such as an interview, with a client or on a panel) and your position and the name of your company.

If your company is a household name such as Apple or Barclays for instance then it would be questioning the audiences intelligence to explain in depth what it is the business does, so share instead an insight into the department you work for or some latest news or information on the business. If a smaller business then this is the opportunity to give a one-line introduction as to what the business does.

Having introduced yourself and your employer, take a moment to succinctly and credibly share an overview on your background and current role and provide context for your presence at the meeting, interview or event – consider discussing its relevance to the latest project you are working on or your objectives for attending. Understand the value proposition that makes you credible in terms of both your experience and achievements as well as capabilities.

While 40 seconds may not sound like much, remember that your 'elevator pitch' is simply a conversation starter and in most instances your audience will interact with questions. It's important therefore to develop an ability to read the tone and direction of the conversation and learn when is the right time to stop talking and ask questions to naturally allow the conversation to develop.

It may, for instance, be the person you are speaking to who enquires about your line of work and what it is your company does – that type of question is a natural opportunity to go into more detail beyond what a 'pitch' would enable.

After successfully pitching yourself, then comes the ability to add stories to bring your message to life. Once again, the old saying 'the best sellers are storytellers' rings true when talking about yourself. Relevant short stories and anecdotes can bring context, humour and interest to a conversation without making it sound like you are talking too much about yourself.

Like anything in life, practice makes perfect, and it's important to gauge reaction and develop your pitch over time whilst avoiding sounding over-rehearsed. As your career evolves so will your pitch. You'll also develop the ability to tailor the message of your pitch to the audience. Preparation and research makes the process of tailoring easier – if you know a little about who your audience are in advance then you can take the time to add interesting stories and personal messaging.

Preparing and practicing your elevator pitch is all part of managing upward and engaging with colleagues at a more senior level. Not only will a little bit of preparation give you additional confidence and help you with your approach and delivery, but it will also give you an upper hand in understanding the background and expectations of the people you are engaging with.

SECTION 4

BIG FIVE TIPS

1. Seek out your organization's leadership competency framework and engage with it. Assess yourself!
2. Show your organization that you are willing to invest in yourself. Own your development.
3. Ensure that you are 'personally' ready to push for your professional goals. Does your personal life support the dedication needed?
4. Be comfortable with who you are – both substance and style.
5. Master the art of articulation, practice brevity of message. Often less is more.

SECTION 5

BE YOURSELF BETTER

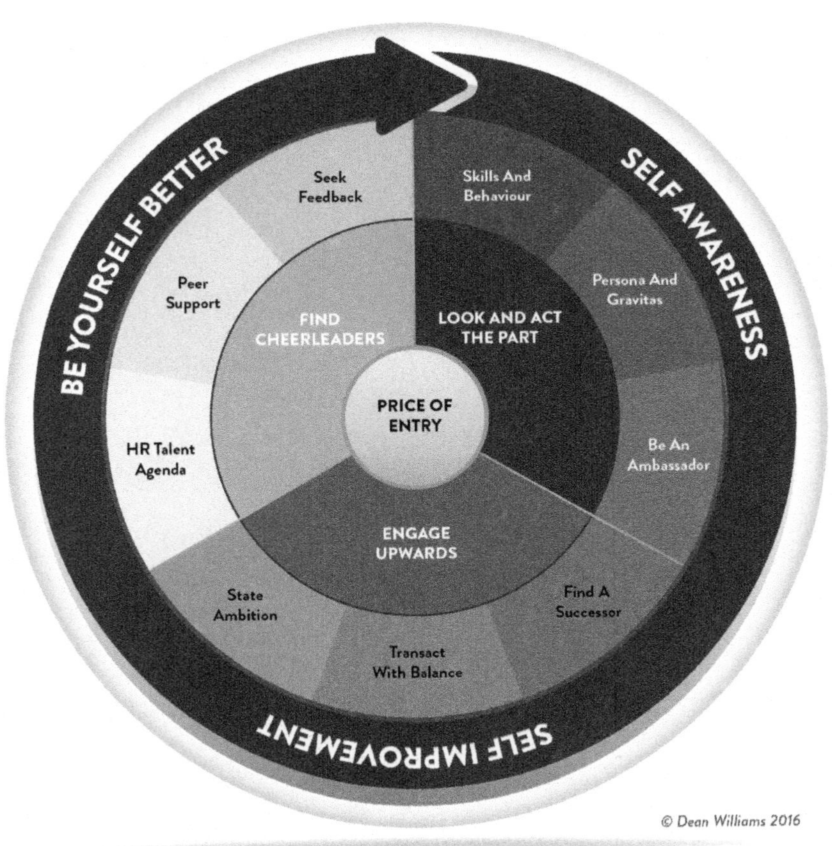

CHAPTER 11
MAKING YOUR MOVE

WHAT TO DO WHEN YOU KNOW YOU ARE READY

Back in Chapter 2, we discussed what you needed to consider, in order to determine whether you were ready to start your push for promotion.

Of course, there are different approaches depending on whether it is an internal or external role you are looking for.

The vast majority of senior appointments are internal – later in this chapter, we will briefly explore how to approach external roles and working with recruitment consultants and headhunters.

Having put in months (if not years) of hard work, actioning the process and advice we give, and building a credible resume, now comes the time for you to formally announce your candidacy for that senior director or executive leadership position.

It may not be a Presidential scale announcement, but it still requires careful consideration, planning and communication.

Consider what immediate value you would bring to the new position, the impact a promotion will have on both your personal and professional life.

By the time you reach this stage of the career ladder, you can be assured that expectations on the candidate are high, just as is the risk for the organization if they get it wrong.

The risks are not just inherent to the organization but to you and your supporters/sponsors.

As we've discussed – relationships – particularly with senior colleagues are critical to get your foot in the door. By this stage, you will almost certainly either have found yourself in a formal talent pool or have been 'sponsored' by a senior executive.

With that degree of exposure, senior leaders will not only be judging your performance but also how you transact at that level.

It is essential at this stage that you are sending out all the right signals that you are ready and that they are being received clearly.

Some of the most obvious signs that you are now ready include:

- You're part of a happy and successful team, in a job that you love and a company you want to work for.
- You have recently been actively mentored by a senior executive or have been part of a formal organizational talent program.
- Senior departmental responsibilities are being routinely passed to you and you're asked to provide cover when your boss is away.
- Your manager, and/or senior managers across the business are consulting you on important decisions or looking to you for solutions.
- You're being invited to more, and higher profile events and meetings.
- You know that your colleagues will be excited about you earning a promotion or making your next career move. If you're moving internally, they will perhaps be excited about working under you in the near future!
- You've built a team and workplace environment where your direct reports will thrive once you move on.
- You've created a clear succession plan for who will replace you in your current role.

By this point in the process your leadership abilities, value to the business and lateral influences across the organization should be well known.

Your ambition is already well known to HR, colleagues and managers and you are making the most of every day, knowing that at some point the right role or opportunity will be yours.

Your network of supporters are in place – your manager and other senior executives are championing your cause.

So, what do you do when that big opportunity arises?

You plan to succeed – nothing is left to chance.

As part of a company talent program, you'll actively be aware (through the course director and mentors) of internal opportunities. For those not participating in a talent pool, announcements will usually come from your manager, HR, a formal mechanism like an online job board or if all else fails via the grape vine.

By comparison, external announcements at director or executive level will almost exclusively come via a recruitment consultant.

The communication channels you've built will ensure you have real-time, first-hand information – keep your ears to the ground as you don't want to be the last to hear about new opportunities.

When a position you are interested in becomes available, then start by requesting a copy of the job description from HR.

Start off, by comparing your skills versus the job description to ensure you are qualified, that you understand the organizational line management structure and to ensure you have sufficient information about the role to enable you to tailor your CV/resume accordingly.

Start planning your application by considering the following factors:

1. Read not only the job description but also research the skills and performance of the departing executive. LinkedIn and departmental reports are a good place to start. Were they held in high regard? What were their major achievements? What traits and characteristics made them stand out?
2. Take the time to review your career history. Your CV doesn't need a full employment history but should rather concentrate on relevant experiences and significant skills and achievements.
3. Assess who else within the organization will be applying for the role and review their strengths and weaknesses. What differentiates you from them? What additional value do you bring to the business?
4. Get in touch with other senior directors and executives and ask questions about what they consider the most essential skills and

experience you need to bring to the job. A good starting point is to ask how would they want to see the successful candidate work with them and their teams?

5. Speak to HR about the application process, including deadlines and presentations. Ask as well about who will be sitting on the interview panel at each stage of the selection process.
6. Based on the job description and the knowledge you have of the role and the people involved, make your case. Every interaction from this point forward is part of the interview process. Use every opportunity to make a lasting positive impression.

As an internal candidate, the informal interview process starts from the moment you communicate your ambition. Every interaction with peers and managers is an opportunity to assert your readiness for that promotion. Whether it is a private one-to-one meeting, an email, a social media post or a networking event, leaders conduct themselves professionally and with balance, knowing that their every move is being scrutinized.

WHAT MAKES INTERNAL CANDIDATES SHINE AT AN INTERVIEW?

With recent research from Wharton Business School showing that external candidates are paid 18% more than internal ones, but performed worse during their first two years in the role – the argument for internal appointments is compelling.

As we have touched on previously, talent professionals know that hiring internal candidates reduces recruiting costs, helps retain high performers and improves company culture.

For those reasons, most director and senior executive level candidates are internal employees who have been carefully nurtured into career advancement positions.

What opening the process up to external candidates does do is enable the position and internal candidates to be compared to the market.

Apart from an outside fresh perspective, one clear advantage which external candidates have, is they are a relative blank canvas. Regardless of your performance or how you believe you are perceived by your colleagues, everyone in your organization will already have an opinion about you.

We've discussed earlier in Chapter 6 about working with your colleagues and peers – cross-organizational knowledge and relationships can help both your reputation as well as prevent people from type casting you in a certain role or leadership style.

Another challenge for internal candidates is that unlike a typical job interview if you are unsuccessful in your application, you still need to return to work with a sense of failure hanging over you. For this reason it is important to time your push for promotion and set parameters of confidentiality regarding your application.

Yes, you have actively communicated your ambition and worked towards promotion but the fact you have applied for a particular role should not always be made public knowledge.

Work with your manager and/or mentor to discuss timings and strategies and set out your aims and objectives.

Follow the same basic steps as any candidate in reviewing the job description and ensuring that this is the right role, at the right time for you and for the business.

If you are confident about proceeding then work with HR to ensure that there is clear and consistent communication from both parties throughout the process. The HR talent team should already be working with you and your manager to advise on upcoming roles and should then guide you through the recruitment process.

All internal candidates should be kept aware of plans to open up the search to external candidates. You should also be made aware of the criteria against which both sets of candidates are being assessed. The benefit of being judged against external candidates is that it increases your credibility when you receive the role – you weren't simply a shoo-in.

At the opposite end of the spectrum, very rarely will an organization may simply wish to appoint an employee without a formal interview process. Whilst this may seem a perfect outcome for you, avoiding the stress and time needed for a formal interview – it can lead to question marks over your future credibility.

In Chapter 12 we will talk more about handling success and failure. Perhaps the biggest challenge for HR talent teams is managing feedback for unsuccessful candidates.

APPLYING FOR EXTERNAL ROLES WITHOUT FEELING LIKE THE OUTSIDER

Most organizations have their senior team in place.

Vacancies are rare, but when they do come up, organizations will scrutinize every candidate to ensure they select the individual who is the right fit.

For the reasons we detailed earlier, being the outsider is difficult. External candidates cost more and statistically have a mixed track record. Fact.

So immediately, most organizations are looking to minimize their risks.

An internal candidate has the advantage of immediate recognition and may have been actively lined up for the role already.

It's up to you to change their mind.

An executive search is about an employer finding the right candidate to lead their business forward and deliver results and growth. Regardless of how exceptional you perceive your own abilities and suitability for a role there will be other external and almost certainly internal candidates who are equally as confident.

You need to demonstrate how being from the outside can bring a fresh perspective, new skills, wider experience or greater diversity to their business and how that can be of benefit to them.

It may sound obvious, but a good starting point is to focus your job search on companies that have a track record of recruiting external executives.

Alternatively, look at companies that are clearly struggling in your specialist field – ones where you know you can offer not just a fresh perspective but also immediate results.

Unlike internal candidacy, which for obvious reasons are primarily handled by HR or more junior roles that increasingly focus on job boards or LinkedIn; most external director and executive opportunities will come from an executive search firm.

Getting yourself in front of these search firms is key to opening up discussions about roles you may be a perfect fit for, but aren't even aware are vacant. Specialist recruiters are often best placed to provide an understanding of the market and your position.

Start off by having a strategy – what is it you want and why? What are your unique selling points and how will you best convey these in a way that demonstrates you are the man or woman for the job?

Like any relationship in business, working with executive recruiters requires groundwork. Some of the simplest ways to get yourself in front of top recruiters and get your name put forward are:

- Have an up to date CV, tailored for a particular role you are interested in.
- Always reply to a recruiters calls or emails, even if the current roles they have are not for you – something more relevant may come along soon.
- Be prepared to answer the basics:
    - o Which companies are you targeting?
    - o What is your unique selling point?
    - o How will you connect with the decision-makers in that organization?
- Make yourself available to meet in person and come prepared with your 'elevator pitch.' Recruiters are normally only compensated upon success, they're working with you, on behalf of their clients – if you fluff your lines, they don't get paid.

As an external candidate, recruiters and employers are working as quickly as possible to get to know you and your value proposition in order to make a decision.

They're looking for candidates with stand out skills and experience who can make an immediate impact in a role, with the minimum of on-boarding and hand-holding. This means that you are both professionally competent but also the right cultural fit for their business.

For these reasons you need to ensure you are creating a consistent and compelling case for them to hire you. You need to communicate your values and objectives.

A professional CV/resume is part of the process, as is your digital footprint. When a recruiter searches for you online, what do they find? Does your online and offline personal brand convey a seamless story of your career?

As part of the process be prepared as well for in depth background and reference checks. Most large corporates today employ specialist data companies to explore your employment history, covering exact dates, pay, education, departmental performance under your tenure, professional memberships, media coverage etc.

You only have to look at the case of Scott Thompson, CEO of Yahoo, who was forced to resign after he lied about his university qualifications from two decades earlier. Honesty and integrity is key – and employers will go out of their way to research your suitability for the role.

MAKING YOUR CV SPEAK FOR ITSELF

By the time you climb the ladder to director or executive level, there are fewer rungs.

Fewer positions becoming available, less frequently, means more competition for places.

What far too many internal candidates fail to understand is the importance of doing the basics well.

They fall in to the trap of believing they are a shoo-in for a role and forget the importance of a well-presented resume, a polished 'elevator pitch' and a strong personal brand.

As with previous chapters, this is not a book about writing the perfect CV or how to prepare for an interview – there are plenty of those out there. But, for completeness, we have included some key points we believe all successful candidates need to focus on.

Remember from the outset that your CV is not just a document focusing on your experience and skills but it is an extension of your personal brand.

Part of the challenge when writing your CV is demonstrating that you can communicate your key messages and achievements succinctly.

One of the biggest flaws with many resumes is that they try to contain too much information, usually because they are simply too generic. Every job application you make requires a new CV, focused on the role you are applying for – your CV is always a work in progress.

What all CV's need to achieve is to communicate the following five things:

1. Articulate your value through your experience and results.
2. Highlight your leadership skills.
3. Present you as a respected and professional individual.
4. Demonstrate you have the ability to communicate and convey a message clearly and succinctly.

5. Show how you are answering the needs of the employer and therefore why you would be the right candidate for this role.

For these reasons, the most effective CV's are those written to directly address the needs of the recruiter. Avoid any irrelevant information that simply makes it more difficult to find answers to the questions they are asking.

For the purposes of brevity, we've divided our top CV tips into four sections; layout, format, length and content.

Whilst content is by far and away the most important, often the first three can be what prevents your CV ever being read.

Layout

- Focus on the information that sits 'above the fold' i.e. the key top third of the first page of your CV. You may have spent hours drafting your CV, but busy recruiters and HR professionals, often spend only a matter of seconds glancing at CV's for the first time. This section needs to catch their eye and contain the most important information.
- Avoid objective headlines such as 'Dynamic professional seeking IT Director level role' and instead, use a title like 'Senior IT Manager.'
- Include your full name, telephone number, email address, links to your social media sites and location so the search firm or employer can contact you easily.
- Include a short introduction summary of two to three lines, to establish your key strengths and latest experience at the outset.
- Start your CV with your employment history, listed in reverse chronological order, including the full name and dates (M/Y) of employment. List beneath in up to three lines your accomplishments. For older or less relevant roles a bullet point will suffice.
- Follow your employment history with a section detailing project history and accomplishments, then education and professional memberships.

Length

- Your CV should be succinct – part of the purpose is demonstrating you can convey a compelling message that captures attention in as few words as possible. Your CV is summarizing your skills and experience.

- To this end, CV's should never be longer than two standard full A4 pages. Why? Because employers don't have the time to sift through pages of information and because most CV's are still printed out and circulated to stakeholders – a double-sided A4 page is more convenient for the reader.

Format

- Your CV should always be formatted in Word and formatted to be easily printed and viewed on any device. The reason? Most executive search firms and HR departments use software to store and search through applications. Whilst a strong design can help your CV stand out from the crowd, ensure this isn't at the cost of being found at all.
- Similarly, stick to traditional fonts such as Times New Roman, and ensure you consistently use font sizes, colours (black) and bold/italics for titles, headers and copy.
- Ensure your CV exactly fills two pages but without squeezing copy onto the page. Consistent spacing is important to ensure flow and ease of reading.
- Many organizations (fewer for senior executive roles) now use LinkedIn as a recruitment tool, which enables you to use your LinkedIn profile and/or a CV. Where possible always opt for a tailored CV but if you have to use LinkedIn ensure you check the formatting of your profile before you submit any applications.

Content

- The content of your CV should always be honest, concise and on-brand. The shorter the copy, the easier it is to read quickly and digest.
- Numbers, percentages and statistics stand out and can help demonstrate your accomplishments but they can also become over-bearing, confusing and at times arrogant so ensure you strike a balance.
- Avoid buzzwords, acronyms and jargon which are both overused by many applicants or may not be familiar to the HR professional reading your CV.
- As already mentioned, you don't need to provide a detailed history of your entire career, focus on your most recent role and relevant experiences. The remainder can simply be bulleted.
- Whilst interests and hobbies can provide an insight about you as a person, they rarely add value on a CV and are often a stock question for interviews.

- Never include information such as your age, gender, family status, etc. – whilst employment law in many countries restricts what can be asked it can also create doubt in an employers mind, if for instance they are looking for you to relocate and they know that would involve moving your whole family. Also, never include a photo; this is a job interview and not a first date.
- Ensure your CV aligns with your 'digital footprint', i.e. does your employment history match your LinkedIn profile?
- And finally, check and double-check your CV for grammatical errors and spelling mistakes. Nothing shows a lack of attention to detail, more than silly mistakes.

MASTERING THE INTERVIEW PROCESS

Getting to the interview stage is something of an achievement in its own right – from amongst what is likely to be dozens if not hundreds of applications, yours is one of a handful deemed sufficiently credible to put in front of the organizations most senior stakeholders.

Consider also, that for the external search firm, as well as the HR professional and manager overseeing the recruitment of the role, there is an element of credibility at stake.

For an internal stakeholder a vacancy creates additional work and can be time consuming and complicated. They are looking for the right person, as soon as possible, to ensure business continuity and a minimal impact upon performance.

They are thus looking to you as a candidate to solve this problem.

It goes without saying therefore, that it is imperative to go into any interview process with a positive attitude, determination and helpfulness. Experience alone won't get you the job you want.

Simply having the skills or experience that match the job description may get you to the interview stage but once in front of a panel it becomes more about value add, cultural fit and ability to thrive and grow in a role. Consider therefore factors such as:

- How can you demonstrate you are a team player?
- What sort of personality are you and how does this fit with the department or team you will be leading?
- How would you deal with specific organizational challenges?
- What additional value do you bring to the role such as networks and contacts?
- Where do you see your next career move taking you after this?
- What do your current manager and colleagues say about you?
- How can the panel best get to know and like you?

There is nothing more off-putting for a potential employer than either arrogance or timidness – if your ego is either a nightmare to work with or you're not confident enough at 'selling' yourself then you'll fall at the first hurdle.

A can-do attitude and ability to think and communicate strategically are key. For that reason, senior leadership level interviews require more preparation and research than managerial positions.

From your CV through to your dealings pre and post interview, every interaction should be structured, clear and professional.

Remember also that practice makes perfect. The less frequently you have been through an interview process, the more room for error.

Far too many senior managers and directors think, that simply because they've interviewed candidates themselves, or 'know their stuff,' that they will be fine in an interview.

Don't make this mistake – there is no substitute for preparedness.

Interviews at different stages of the process also take many different forms. With teams now spread globally, Skype and Web Chats are commonplace, even for the most senior of positions.

This type of 'virtual' interview can be entirely alien to many people who are not used to the technical aspects or dynamics of video conferencing.

Our top tips for preparing for interview are:

1. Work with the HR professional or recruitment consultant to get as much information as possible about the role, organization and panel. Ask questions about:
   - The overall process – how many stages, what are the likely timings; how will they convey feedback etc?
   - Style of the interview – will the interview be online, a technical interview, involve a presentation?
   - Make up of the panel – who will be conducting the panel and links to their profiles?
   - Specifics of the interviews – time, date and place?
2. Research the company, competitors and industry trends in depth. In an increasingly global world, you will need to be familiar with regional and market-based focuses, organizational structures and core products and services.

3. Ensure you have reviewed your CV thoroughly before the interview – most interviewers will have a copy in front of them and will base their questioning from what you have already told them. Your interview should be an expansion of the personal brand story you've told on paper.
4. Do your background research on the interviewer or panel members. Break preparation down into small tasks. The easiest place to start is with LinkedIn and on the company website. Most senior executives will have a detailed bio online and links to their social media profiles and any thought leadership interviews, articles or blogs – which is a great way to understand what they are talking about and are interested in. Look for shared interests, which you can use as conversation starters, while also keeping an eye out for things to avoid discussing if they clearly have a strong negative view on a topic.
5. Prepare and perfect your elevator pitch. You only get one chance at making a first impression (you've seen that before in this book) and within the first 15 to 30 seconds of an interview a decision can already be made. One of the main mistakes that candidates make is not to relax and enjoy the opportunity – presenting the interviewer with a smile, relaxed greeting and firm handshake sets the tone for a positive interview and gives you the platform from which to 'sell yourself'. Remember to strike the balance between gravitas and warmth – remember the reason you are putting yourself through the process is to get a job, so you need to make the panel want to see you again and work with you in future.
6. Remember that you are selling your story and your personal brand, so ensure you are interesting, likable and are providing insights into you as a person. We've all had experience of candidates who have been a perfect fit for a role, performed well at interview but have been told that the panel felt they were 'too polished' and that they didn't get a sense of them as a person. Sometimes being over prepared can be a hindrance, instead prepare relevant stories and anecdotes that highlight your career success stories.
7. Interviewing someone you know is usually never easy. If you are an internal interviewee consider the following:
    - Ask the HR coordinator about any rules or how they'd like to handle the interview.
    - Always be friendly, informal and yet professional with someone you know well.

- The interviewer may already be familiar with your work history, while others on the panel may not be. It may, therefore, be helpful to start by stating that for completeness you will be covering some information that they may already know. Assume they know nothing.

Internal candidates...don't cut corners in the interview process. An external candidate won't – you will need to, at least, match their approach. Assume nothing.

8. Be prepared for tough questions about your career history and track record. Never become defensive or unsettled, instead take the time to calmly and confidently explain your position – ultimately you know the background of your career better than anyone. Be prepared to connect your answers to examples of how you have used your skills to deliver results using real stats and information – avoid general statements at all costs. Remember to have a key point that you want to make and push home the message, highlighting your uniqueness.
9. Don't be alarmed by 'odd-ball questions'. Whilst less common in director level interviews, many firms often throw in seemingly bizarre questions as a way of testing a candidates critical thinking skills. Putting them on the spot, shows how an interviewee in real-time and whilst thinking out loud, navigates a question and provides a solution. These are just some examples of such questions:
   - "How lucky are you and why?" – Airbnb, Content Manager.
   - "If you were a pizza delivery man, how would you benefit from scissors?" –Apple, Specialist.
   - "Are you more of a hunter or a gatherer?" – Dell, Account Manager.
   - "You're a new addition to the crayon box, what colour would you be and why?" – Urban Outfitters Sales Associate.
   - "How does the Internet work?" – Akamai, Director.
10. Prepare insightful questions to ask the interviewer or panel that enable you to demonstrate your knowledge of the company and industry and to garner additional insight into expectations about performance and the role. Examples include:
    - "What does success look like in the first 60 to 90 days?" – this question gives you insight into the priorities and expectations of

your future manager/employer and allows you to respond with ways in which you can help them achieve an immediate impact.

- "What attributes do your star performers share?" – not only are you positioning yourself as a potential top performer but you gain insight in to the panels expectations of key skills and qualities.
- "What do you see as the major challenges to growth within the company over the next 6–12 months?" – be it talent acquisition, technology, competitor advantage or economic uncertainty, asking directly about the challenges the business faces will enable you to better focus on how you can bring value to the organization.
- "How would you describe the company culture and working here?" – for external candidates, this question enables you to get an insight into what the panel perceive are the most important aspects of the company culture and their personal feelings about the working environment.

After an interview it is important to continue a constant positive stream of contact with the HR professional administrating the process. A thank you note and a request for information on timings for feedback will help you understand what to expect next.

WHERE DO YOU EXPECT TO BE IN FIVE YEARS TIME?

We've talked a lot about the importance of planning a road map for your career – this is far more about helping to articulate your ambition and deliver immediate results as it is about setting long-term career objectives, which frankly can change at any time.

Individuals with clear, written goals, are proven to accomplish far more in the short-term, even if the longer-term ambition is more flexible.

There's no surprise then that the question, "where do you expect to be in five years time?" has become a firm favourite with employers. For an organization, it is not just about your ambition but also whether they can expect you to commit to the role you are targeting – or, is this simply a stepping-stone?

We've included this short section as both a re-cap but also to ensure you understand how to best articulate your ambition. The 'five-year question' is also far more complicated than at first glance; what it's really asking is a series of questions:

- Can you communicate the extent of your ambition?
- What are your long-term career objectives and goals?
- How quickly do you view the development and progression process?
- Is your next job simply a stepping-stone in your career and does that pose a risk?
- What are you looking for both in your professional and personal life?
- What does success look like for you?

Understanding the company culture and approach to talent management will help you to align with the personal qualities the organization is looking for.

It is important to recognize that the primary role of HR professionals is not to assist you with your career ambition but to protect the organization. HR departments will seek to ensure that candidates have a growth mind-set and that they are highly motivated towards the immediate position.

Whilst country HR teams drive talent strategy; it is the C-suite at a global level who control your future, using their authority and seniority to push your prospects.

They are looking for three signs:

1. Is the individual going to take any job offer at any organization or does this role align with both their immediate skill-levels and long-term ambition in a way that would be mutually beneficial?
2. Does the individual transact with balance in such a way that his mind-set and persona align with the organizations talent agenda and prove that they are sufficiently capable of performing so as not to pose a risk either to the organization or to the credibility of the senior executive supporting them?
3. Have they identified a potential successor? Have they demonstrated an understanding that leadership is also about mentorship, legacy and creating continuity? Consider this; are you too good at what you do to lose you? If you haven't developed a strong succession plan – employers may consider keeping you where you are, rather than risk losing your skills/impact in a given critical role, even if the promotion is an internal one.

For candidates it is important to demonstrate a willingness to invest time in their professional development as well as recognizing transferable skills that bring an immediate value to the organization.

You must bring energy and emotional intelligence to every interaction and engagement – positivity generates positive thinking not just for you, but in your peers, making you more aware to the options and opportunities around you.

Breaking free from your comfort zone demonstrates an ability to expand your boundaries and to react to change. Pushing your boundaries opens new possibilities which you would otherwise not gain access to.

When considering any push for promotion, explore the job market and consider your options. Identify the types of role you want, document your achievements and show how you have delivered business results in your current role.

Being considered talented in your field is simply not enough, it will only open the door. Performing on the 'big stage' in a manner which instils trust and confidence is what will get you noticed.

But remember, no leader is ever entirely complete. Nerves are normal and skill-gaps can be filled. Identifying and taking constructive feedback on areas of potential weakness is a key trait of leadership.

CHAPTER 12

DEALING WITH SUCCESS AND FAILURE

GIVING AND RECEIVING BAD NEWS

Setbacks come in all shapes and sizes.

Failure also means different things to different people, and we will all make mistakes and experience failure in our careers (most of us many times).

We may be passed over for a promotion; fail to close an important deal or see our startup venture fail to take-off.

At the moment they happen, setbacks can be devastating – but they shouldn't be destructive if you manage them correctly.

As managers and leaders, we are also likely to be on the giving and not just receiving end of bad news. How we manage and communicate difficult situations is not only a key business skill but a benchmark against which we are judged. Your ability to do this well is one of the indicators for promotion readiness.

Having difficult conversations and facing up to uncertainty will be part of what defines us both, as a leader and in our next career steps.

We talked earlier in Chapter 7 about delivering feedback to your team, but one of the trickiest situations for any organization or employee is when an internal candidate fails in the latter stages of a job interview.

Unlike interviewing for an external role, if you fail to get an internal promotion you still have to get up the next day and go to work at the same office.

There are lessons here to be learned for any business person – whether you work in HR, are the manager delivering the feedback, or are on the receiving end.

Consider also that bad news doesn't just apply to weak or average employees.

Sometimes even highly valued members of your team will fail and how that feedback is delivered can have a huge bearing on a candidate's future with the company.

If you are the candidate on the receiving end of bad news, how that feedback is delivered will have immediate implications on your short and longer-term future.

Decisions are taken for business reasons and should not be taken personally. It's going to be a huge disappointment, but there will be other opportunities.

Your immediate focus is on limiting any negative impact, learning from the experience and ensuring your longer-term future.

Forward-thinking organizations understand that clear communication and transparency is the key to ensuring the candidate remains a valued member of the company.

For anyone delivering feedback and advice they need to deliver this type of information with skill, emotional intelligence and sincerity. An unsuccessful candidate is feeling vulnerable, disappointed and acutely aware of how they may be being perceived – i.e. they can see through any BS.

As a manager, you will likely have had to prepare to deliver bad news to your direct reports before. It is key that you prepare for the discussion and sense check the information you will be giving them and ask yourself:

- What outcomes would be the most positive/productive?
- How composed do I feel? The unsuccessful candidate is likely to be disappointed or angry – therefore, as the person giving the feedback, you need to be in emotional control.

Pay attention to how you as a manager relay bad news – and your expectations of how your direct reports would react. If you were placed in the situation of being the unsuccessful candidate, how would you be able to accept bad news?

Consider the following advice:

- Arranging a face-to-face meeting with the unsuccessful candidate to explain why they did not get the job or promotion they applied for, explain why other candidates more closely fitted the brief.
- Be ready to explain 'why' using relevant examples of where their experience may not have matched the skills needed for the role.
- Be honest, don't avoid the issue and ensure you are clear and transparent.
- Listen more than you talk. Disappointment may mean the unsuccessful candidate is not bursting with questions but inside they are likely to be in a state of turmoil.
- Re-iterate that the candidate was highly thought of and had a realistic chance of getting the job but finished behind a candidate who better fitted the skills the business was looking for, for that particular role.
- Convey to the candidate that it was a hard search and a tough decision and they should be proud of making it that far.
- Reassure the candidate that they are valued by the business and have a future despite this setback.
- You should work with the unsuccessful candidate to create a privacy plan that provides just enough information into the public domain, so as to explain why they were not suitable for the role, without damaging that individual's reputation or ego.
- Discuss their positive strengths and how they can grow and perform, both more successfully in their current role and gain more relevant experience.
- Reassure the candidate that there are future opportunities for advancement.
- If the candidate is particularly important and likely to feel negative, consider lining up an alternative high profile project for them to move straight into.
- Agree with the unsuccessful candidate how much information will be shared with the person who has the new job, ensuring they have a smooth working relationship.
- Support them – and deliver on your promises.

What you should avoid doing is:

- Delaying or wavering. The approach and decision must be clear and consistent with past like for like scenarios.
- Creating additional confusion by over-complicating the issue.
- Blaming either the candidate or anyone else involved in the process for the failure.
- Dodging having difficult conversations or providing upfront feedback. Make time for face-to-face discussion.
- Getting defensive or emotional, especially if the candidate does.
- Talking too much – balance answering questions with listening to what the unsuccessful candidate has to say.
- Embarrassing the candidate. Agree on options for privacy and a strategy for helping them develop in future.

For candidates receiving the bad news, clearly it is likely to be a very disappointing time.

Unsuccessful candidates are advised to take the following immediate steps, before considering the longer-term career implications:

- Take a deep breath and remove emotion from the equation. Promotion decisions are taken for business and not personal reasons. Acting impulsively or in anger can both damage relationships as well as say to an employer that they were right to not give you the promotion after all.
- Thank the panel and HR team conducting the search and ask for formal feedback. Ideally, this should be face-to-face so that you can ask questions and explore how you can continue to develop within the company and your current role.
- Speak to your close circle of supporters to help you evaluate where you think you went wrong and what can be changed for next time.

HANDLING CAREER SETBACKS

"I have missed more than 9,000 shots in my career. I have lost almost 30 games. On 26 occasions I have been entrusted to take the game winning shot, and I missed. I have failed over and over and over again in my life. And that is why I succeed." Michael Jordan

Let's avoid the clichés – losing sucks!

Unfortunately, however, failure is part of life, and we should view it as a bruise and not a scar.

Whilst we talk of career ladders, few are linear. Everyone stumbles occasionally – successful leaders/executives just don't make it a habit.

When you get the bad news that you haven't got the promotion you wanted, you cannot let the disappointment impact upon either your current performance or your longer-term career.

What you need to do is act.

Doing nothing won't resolve the situation.

Take a moment to pause and gather your emotions. Avoid burning bridges with impulsive or emotional reactions. While at this point you can't turn things around, you can make the situation far worse by acting inappropriately. Consider the following risks:

- Making a huge issue out of the decision could risk alienating colleagues (and supporters). There is also a risk you could come across as an individual whose career ambitions exceed their ability.
- Don't get upset or burn bridges – you never know when you'll need those relationships in future. Having a meltdown and resigning may feel cathartic but will that type of behaviour either get you a new job or a glowing reference – we doubt it!
- Bringing emotion and anger into the situation often demonstrates immaturity. This type of behaviour often serves to prove doubters right in not appointing you.

We talked a moment ago about the immediate actions you should take in terms of receiving feedback and agreeing next steps – but then what?

Start off by thinking about what you need to do to achieve positive outcomes in future applications.

Failure taken in perspective is an opportunity to learn. Act upon feedback without replaying it over and over again in your head.

Understand where you came up short. Was it the wrong role? Did you lack experience in a key skill? Did you under perform at interview?

Analyze what went well – take the positives from your performance and decide how you can keep these front and centre of the organizations mind.

Your response is divided into two equal halves – psychological and action driven. The psychology is often the least considered but the most important. Start by:

- Accepting that you have failed in this instance and move on. Blaming your failure on 'bad luck,' a conspiracy theory or simply getting yourself into a state of depression won't help. You lost out – it happens – get over it.
- As legendary coach, Vince Lombardi said, "*The greatest accomplishment is not in never falling, but in rising again after you fall.*" Failure helps develop perseverance, teaches determination, shows character and resilience and forces us to analyze and improve our own performance.
- Reframing your failure as a tough but necessary learning experience is a useful first step in broadening your skills and experiences in order to better match future requirements. Use every opportunity to learn more.
- Failure also forces leaders to take responsibility. To accept that the buck stops with them and that they have the skills necessary to succeed in future.

Then comes the actions – those must do's which demonstrate that you have picked yourself off the ground and are ready to push on. These include:

- Start off by planning your next steps, in particular, any obstacles or difficult/embarrassing conversations that may crop up. A rehearsed answer and clear mind will demonstrate that you are in the right frame of mind to move on and grow.

- Gathering feedback from both the interview panel, your manager and supporters whilst ensuring you listen and don't get defensive. Consider also speaking with a recruitment consultant to get an understanding of skills and opportunities across the industry.
- Remember to keep a positive outlook – just because you're disappointed doesn't mean you can exude it. As a manager and leader, you need to remain positive or risk impacting the mood of your whole team or company.
- If a lack of relevant experience or skills let you down then work with HR to gain exposure and training, so you don't find yourself in that situation again. Asking for this type of exposure at this time is likely to be met with a positive response – HR will be keen to soften the blow of rejection and retain your skills. Consider if there are any special projects or a lateral job move that could help your exposure and change perceptions of your experience.
- Speak to HR about the successful candidate and reach out to congratulate them and discuss how best you can support them in future.
- Thank your support network for their efforts and request their advice and feedback. Listen to any stories they have about dealing with setbacks and consider reading up on great business leaders who regularly write about their career or product failures and how they overcame them.
- Finally, consider getting a business coach who can help you through the process – can facilitate feedback and offer support and guidance on your next steps.

Above all else, remember that failure to get the promotion you want is simply a short-term setback. How you manage that setback will have a far greater impact on your long-term future than the result will.

The process of getting back up after a career stumble is as important and defining as winning is. Like with every part of our journey together, planning for success, even in moments of defeat is important to reaching a measured and sustainable outcome.

DEALING WITH SUCCESS AND YOUR COLLEAGUES

At the other end of the spectrum is success.

You've worked long and hard to earn the promotion or appointment that you wanted – now is the time to pause for five minutes, savour the moment and then seize the opportunity.

Success is often more about the recognition you give yourself than it is the praise of others.

The best leaders, however, are humble but authoritative. They don't dwell on their success, and they certainly aren't boastful – at some point, you'll fail yourself.

For many leaders, whilst promotion above their peers is something they've worked hard for, it can also be a very stressful experience.

It's important in this regard to remember you will likely be working alongside candidates who you have beaten to the role. In this instance, it is important to work with HR in ensuring a degree of privacy and a firm working relationship with those colleagues. Within what follows, we'll explore how to approach day one in your new role.

If you are an external candidate then there are other things to consider:

- You may have been appointed over an internal candidate – how will the team and individual react and embrace you?
- You need to set about learning the company culture, understanding organizational structure and building personal relationships.

All this while building momentum and delivering performance.

In order to transition into your new role you should consider:

- What this new role means to you and what type of a leader/director you see yourself being?
- How will the appointment help you reach your longer-term objectives? What skills and experience will it give you?
- What will this position enable you to do in terms of obtaining results?
- What will the impact be on your work/life balance?

The challenge then becomes managing your own expectations and how you most effectively manage your own time and delegate work to your team.

When it comes to managing a new team – especially a team who used to be your co-workers – you need to remember that the balance of the relationship has permanently changed.

Whilst friendships and relationships should be sustained, your position demands professionalism, transparency and clarity of decision-making. No decision or action can be clouded by doubts about your previous loyalties or relationships.

But at the same time, successful leaders and directors understand the importance of consistency, continuity and most importantly two-way communication.

We all want to make an impact, but sustainable career success (as we discuss in the next Chapter) is built upon solid decision making – not spectacular change and disruption for the sake of it.

Some of the key actions that we have seen from leaders who get it right include:

- Sit down with your team members one on one and as a team and ask them what they think is and isn't working in the business. Challenge them on their short and long term personal aims and objectives and understand what drives them and how you can support them.
- Be clear about your expectations of performance and conduct, and be clear and assertive in your communications.
- Ensure that you delegate effectively based upon ability and experience, not upon past friendships. Any sign of favouritism will stir discontent.
- Communicate your passion, energy and vision for the role in a way that inspires your new team to support you.
- Let your team understand your working style and how you can best work together for mutual benefit and individual success.
- At the same time manage expectations and concerns at the start. Lofty targets and demands can be unsettling for a team – keep your expectations realistic yet challenging and set out how you will support your team in reaching them.

- Reach out to other managers and departments and keep them engaged with your plans. Ask them for their advice, input and requirements and how you can best support them to reach their objectives.

Consider also the support mechanisms you need to put in place to ensure your own success.

Do you have a clear understanding of your objectives, KPIs, major projects and key stakeholders?

Without the right support network to monitor and review your own progress you are unlikely to be able to build the sustained results and momentum needed for future career growth.

COMMUNICATING YOUR SUCCESS

Appointing a new director or senior executive is a big deal for most organizations and particularly the teams they'll be leading.

For you, it'll be one of the most exciting and challenging times of your personal and professional life.

Great leaders work hard to build both credibility and momentum from the outset.

You should take steps to prepare both emotionally, in your personal life and professionally in terms of your research and planning for your new role.

Make the use of any down time between accepting an offer and starting a position to give yourself the best chance of succeeding.

Whilst you should respect people and processes that are already in place, you should arrive with your own ideas – ready to engage, challenge and drive progress.

The business has the responsibility to successfully position you as a new director – it's in their best interests.

News of a senior appointment travels quickly.

Most announcements need planning, in order to manage the expectations of your new team, employees across the organization and any external stakeholders such as clients. **You'll be amazed by how frequently the incoming leader is asked to put together their own announcement! So with that in mind ...**

Consider the logistics of who should know what about your appointment (and when)?

- What message are you sending out about the aims and vision of the business with this appointment?
- How will the announcement impact any unsuccessful internal candidates and your new team?

- Why are you the right person for the job and what information about you should be shared?
- Who, both internally and externally needs to be informed?
- When, and in what order should they be notified?
- By whom and through what medium should they be told?

Regardless of how well you plan your message, you can't get around the fact that employees and stakeholders will all have their own ideas and opinions of who should have been appointed.

It is important therefore to manage the process and people reactions carefully by taking into account that an announcement is likely to result in different reactions in different teams and departments.

Ask yourself and consider the following;

- Have you spelt out the strategic rationale and time frames for the appointment?
- Have you considered the impact your appointment will have on other team members – not just unsuccessful candidates? Are there relationships that will need re-examining to avoid the risk of losing talent?
- Have you considered how to reach out and communicate with an unsuccessful candidate on your team?

Ensure your initial announcement strikes a balance between continuity and certainty, whilst leaving you with sufficient room to develop and deliver your own strategies.

You should always keep external stakeholders informed about your commitment to maintaining and enhancing the business value and vision.

Consider too the best way of breaking the news. A senior appointment in a large organization may need to be simultaneously announced to shareholders, staff and the press via a press release but in a smaller organization, a team meeting may have more of the personal touch.

While emails are a convenient and transparent way of notifying a wide audience they can also appear functional and fail to convey the importance of the appointment.

However, you decide to make the announcement you need to remember that it will set the tone for your first days and even months in the role. You have a tough enough task on hand as it is – giving yourself a platform to build and lead from is key.

CHAPTER 13

EXCEEDING EXPECTATIONS

THE HIGHER YOU CLIMB THE STEEPER IT GETS

As you climb the career ladder, so the skills that enabled you to thrive in your early career and that earned you the right to a promotion, will no longer be the same skills that will make you a success in a senior leadership/executive role.

Increasingly, you will find yourself judged upon your understanding of the business, ability to lead, inspire teams and most importantly your ability to communicate a sense of vision to stakeholders at every level.

Like anything in life, success favours the prepared.

From the moment you make the decision to accelerate your career ambition, you should begin planning for success – not just in terms of meeting expectations placed upon you but consistently exceeding them.

As a director or C-Level executive, you are expected to not-only lead departments and support the CEO on overall organizational strategy but to contribute your own insights and to make key decisions.

Whether your promotion was internal or you have moved to an entirely new company, it is in your employers best interests to position you for success.

You've announced your arrival, credentials and remit to the organization. Now comes the greatest challenge of your career – proving your worth.

You need to demonstrate why you were the best person for the role and thereby repay the faith that the selection panel placed in your abilities.

And, whilst it is reasonable to allow any new starter time to understand the business and build relationships, be under no illusions, expectations are for immediate results.

How immediate are we talking? Quite simply, from day one.

Conventionally we divide performance into one week, one month, three months and one-year sprints.

Starting off on the front foot means having a 90-day action plan and the ability to evolve your plan as your knowledge and relationships grow.

Never underestimate the importance of the on-boarding process. From pre-start, through to the end of your first week, your focus should be on understanding the business challenges faced by your customers and your people.

Focus on the three key areas: people, strategy and results.

During the first week, it is important not to lose sight of why you were successful in getting your new role and what is expected of you.

While you may be settling into the role, do not forget you are still being interviewed. With probation periods usually no less than three to six months, every day is like an interview.

Go back to your job description and even interview questions to ensure you understand what is expected of you and what you've promised you will deliver.

Whilst we all know job descriptions hardly reflect what we do in our daily roles, what they do reflect is what your boss wanted from someone filling the role you now occupy.

Small things matter, so think about how to:

- Ask questions – particularly obvious ones – during these first few weeks you have the excuse of being new. Ask a silly question in a months time and you'll look like you're out of your depth.

- Get some quality time in the diary with your senior colleagues and your team, with the explicit aim of setting expectations. Align your objectives with theirs and work towards ensuring you all agree what success looks like over the first week, month and three month sprints.
- Get yourself organized from the get go – following up every meeting with a thank you and an email summary of action points. Spend time planning your day and turn up for meetings on time and properly prepared.
- Ensure you get out and get seen. Once the day one niceties are done, then comes the follow up necessity of ensuring you are seen and heard in all the right places. This doesn't just mean senior meetings but also those where you can add expert guidance.
- Take the time to check-in with your existing network and update them on your new role. Use the opportunity to ask them for personal references and any tips or insights that can help you in your new role.

Small gestures can also make a big impact. Making time to meet not just your team and senior colleagues but also staff on the ground. Speak to staff who interact everyday with your customers or clients and elicit their thoughts, and opinions. Why not volunteer for a shift on a customer service support centre or go out into the field with a sales rep?

Such efforts can set the tone for the type of leader you want to be seen as.

BUILD LASTING RELATIONSHIPS WITH STAKEHOLDERS

It's important from the outset to get to know your internal and external stakeholders and, in particular, their business and personal objectives, the challenges they face and their vision of what success looks like.

At this stage in any new role, it's about making first impressions count and behaving and conducting yourself to the level of your role. Approach every conversation with confidence, warmth, interest and gravitas.

A good start is by being visible and allocating time to get out and meet people – both colleagues and clients. Make an effort to understand the structure of the team and organization and meet and communicate with key stakeholders, be it in a formal meeting or over coffee.

When it comes to external stakeholders – clients/customers, shareholders, the general public – it's important to remain patient, focusing on a core message of competence.

- Get to know their business, where they fit into the structure and their key objectives. Approach your first meetings with a strong understanding of their objectives and challenges and those of the wider industry. Come fully briefed on the account history and all current and upcoming milestones.
- Arrive with the aim to make an impactful first impression. For larger key clients, consider securing an additional value-add from your company that you can offer up to the client to demonstrate the value you too will place on the account.
- Ensure you reach out and make the first contact with key accounts and maintain that level of engagement throughout the relationship. Never forget the importance of acknowledging communications and replying promptly to emails – a prompt response will let your client know that you are focused on them and their business.
- Follow up all meetings and calls with an email or contact report detailing the discussion and setting out next steps and responsibilities for any actions. Always ask the client to provide any feedback or amends to your notes.

When meeting with internal stakeholders, take the opportunity to understand the company culture as well as getting to know them as an individual and their interests, passions and personal situation outside of the office.

Each and every business is different, so take time to identify star performers and the behaviours that set them apart from the rest. Pay particular attention to where and how they have achieved recognition and consider if there are ways to apply the same formulae to your approach.

If you're new to the business or even the team, then use these initial conversations to establish the rules and working patterns, such as who works from home? How do colleagues like to communicate – email, calls, VC or IM? Where do colleagues go for a drink after work? Who controls access to meeting rooms? They may sound like simple things, but they can be major hurdles to productivity during your early days.

Most people's diaries fill up days, if not weeks in advance so don't waste a moment in getting some face time with your new colleagues.

Follow-up both informal or formal meetings with an email or better still connect with people on LinkedIn – which enables you to keep a record of names and faces while also giving these stakeholders a subtle way to learn more about your experience and expertise.

Building new professional relationships can be challenging and time-consuming. The change of work environment, responsibility and sometimes industry, will test your resilience. It's important to keep things in perspective – you'll be expected to bring immediate value to the business in terms of ideas and energy, but you cannot be expected to know everything and deliver change on day one.

True leaders avoid being drawn into negative conversations. In times of change, emotions can be high and colleagues can be quick to confide in the new person. Manage conversations and in particular emails, being careful to avoid not being seen as/or siding with a complainer.

At the same time, there will be expectations and judgments placed upon you – placing the blame on your predecessor or team only comes across as being defensive.

FOCUS ON OPERATIONAL EXCELLENCE

Taking on any new role means new challenges – some will be familiar and some entirely alien. It's your responsibility to make the transition as seamless as possible and to deliver operational effectiveness immediately.

At the same time, your teams will be expecting you to begin detailing the future strategy, vision and direction of things to come.

Whilst life goes on regardless of a new director or executive; you will quickly need to stamp your own style on the way your teams operate. Start off with a focus on:

- Strategy – give your team and senior colleagues an early insight into where your focus and objectives lie and a clear time frame for delivering your first strategy.
- People – build the foundations of a solid functioning team by establishing not only core skills but also where an individuals' passion and desire to contribute sit.
- Results – set out clearly what is expected of your team and the KPIs they will be reporting against.

Meet with your team of direct reports early and often, to understand their ambitions and start shaping them into the team you need to deliver on your vision. Not every team you inherit will have the right people or mix of skills so use the first two to three months to ensure you have the right team around you – and that the right people are in the right roles.

Just because you inherit a structure and team doesn't mean there is not scope to change things around, many employees will jump at the opportunity for a new challenge or to broaden their skillsets. At the same time, set about building a working environment that enables your team to operate at a higher level, one where communication and innovation can thrive.

It is important to pay attention to detail. You can be forgiven for not knowing everything about your new role, but what you do execute on needs to be high quality. All eyes will be on you, both from above and the team around you so conduct yourself with confidence and where possible, practice and sense-check every statement and decision.

Seek out opportunities to differentiate yourself from your predecessor. Demonstrating a grasp of the business is one thing, proving that you add another level of value will help you stand out. Even small points, such as arriving at work early, stepping in to support existing projects and bringing fresh ideas on communication and collaboration can all make an impact to the business.

Whilst we've already discussed the importance of getting out and meeting people early and often, it is also important to manage your time. Whether you are new to the organization or moving up the ladder, you are likely to be in demand – expect colleagues to want to connect, engage, try and build relationships and be naturally interested in your objectives and strategies.

You've been appointed to bring about change, so consider where efficiencies can be made.

Leaders have a grasp on four key fundamentals, the needs of their clients, the capabilities of their teams, an in-depth knowledge of their budget and an acute understanding of the data and analytics behind the business. Start by aligning budgets with client needs and establishing what is critical and what is not.

Every leadership transition needs to bring with it a sense of closure and forward progression, so make time to bury the bodies of leftover legacy. Focus on what are the necessary day to day activities that need to continue, as well as on less critical projects being led by your predecessor which may not align with your new strategy or feature as a priority.

Keep your message simple and ensure that colleagues understand and can themselves effectively communicate it to others. The more senior your new role, the greater the impact it will have on the business. During the early days expect a degree of excitement, intrigue and skepticism. With so many contrasting mind-sets, clear and simple communication is vital – less is more and simplicity and clarity of language is key to removing doubt. Keep it short and visual – no long work documents.

Ensure you consistently reinforce your successes. There is a fine line between bragging about your achievements and letting those around you know that you are bringing immediate results to the business. Starting a presentation with a recap of key objectives and recent wins is a good way to keep your team on track with their targets and at the same time reinforce that you're delivering results in line with those KPIs.

In summary, consider these three critical factors:

- Understand the business, its vision and objectives and where you can add value.
- Ensure you understand the needs of all stakeholders, their objectives and challenges.
- Establish how you can make a big impact without full-scale change or excessive expenditure – where are the easy wins? Don't be afraid however to spend money in order to increase efficiency, so long as there is a clear ROI.

EXECUTE WITH PRECISION AND POISE

"Productivity is never an accident. It is always the result of a commitment to excellence, intelligent planning, and focused effort." Paul J. Meyer

If planning is the foundation of success, then execution is the entire structure that sits upon those foundations. No degree of knowledge and expertise, or slick presentations will make up for poor execution.

Therefore, planning should not be just about your grand vision and ideas, but about the details of how you will achieve those objectives in an efficient, effective and impactful way.

Executing projects – both big and small – with precision and composure will demonstrate your ability to get the job done. Keep budgets and timelines in mind and avoid the temptation for complete change – upsetting the apple cart poses unnecessary risks with little reward. Set about instead understanding what works and what doesn't and the tweaks that are needed. If things are being done in a particular way, it is likely it is for a reason, so never assume you know better.

Quick wins can be highly impactful, showcasing your core skills and ability to align and inspire teams to work with you.

Remember that executing with precision is not just about exceptional outcomes; some projects just need someone to make it happen. Think therefore in terms of what the MVP is – the Minimum Value Proposition – what is the very least you can do to deliver the right result? You may not want to hang it on your CV but sometimes you need to be the person to make it happen.

A good place to start is a gap analysis – this research element will enable you to better understand your role, the challenges the business faces and where short and long term capability gaps exist.

Use this research to develop a written three month plan, focused on challenges, objectives, deliverables and KPIs. Work with your team and senior colleagues when developing your gap analysis, both to seek their engagement and buy in, as well as to clearly set out what you are going to be focusing on. Consider the WHY? HOW? And WHAT? approach to planning.

From your gap analysis, expand this into a list of key actions – ideally between five and ten objectives that you commit to achieve during this initial introduction period. Take the time to write them down in order of priority or chronologically, based upon delivery, while articulating what value they will bring the business. Use this template to brief colleagues on progress and make a big deal of when they are completed and signed-off.

Create projects for you and your team – it's a great way of securing wins and fostering teamwork. In the process, this teamwork will allow you to learn more about the strengths, weaknesses and behaviours of your team.

Spend time at the start, considering not only what comes next, but what the impact of your changes will be and how you maximize the positive outcomes or minimize the negative risk. This is one of the clearest ways in which high achievers differentiate themselves from the crowd – they have an ability to calculate the impact of their actions and to think three moves beyond their current actions.

Successful directors and executives continually raise the bar for themselves and their teams. Inspiring and challenging your team to achieve at a higher level can often be tough – it's worth therefore setting out your expectations early on.

Don't be afraid to make use of all your assets – leverage your old contacts and processes from previous roles to add value and insight. Make it in others best interests to help you succeed.

Take time to consider your impact by asking the following questions:

- Are you actually making a difference?
- Do senior colleagues listen to you and engage with your vision?
- How have you raised the performance and sales numbers across the business, your department, or among your team of direct reports?

- Are your agreed personal KPIs aligned with the business – do you have P&L responsibility?
- Have you been tasked to lead business critical projects?

Be clear as to what a positive impact looks like. Is it a definable KPI or metric? Have you seen an increase in revenue, an increase in brand awareness or share of voice in the market? Are your employees more engaged or collaborating more effectively? Or have you perhaps managed to reduce costs or enhance efficiency? What was your role in achieving this success and how can you most effectively articulate this so that you are associated both with the actions and the results?

GROW YOUR PROFESSIONAL CONFIDENCE AND CONVERSATIONAL IQ (C-IQ)

True gravitas comes from your ability to balance emotional and conversational intelligence and to make a lasting impact every time you engage with people.

For it's part, Conversational Intelligence (C-IQ) is our ability to connect and engage with stakeholders in such a way that builds trust and lasting relationships. Conversations are not simply about sharing information, but how we connect, navigate and grow.

It is what enables leaders to communicate their vision in such a way as to inspire their people to work with them to achieve results – to build trust through co-creating conversations and making your vision and objectives a shared outcome.

No leader, regardless of how talented can achieve their objectives without a team. When leaders engage with others, value their suggestions and inspire new thinking they create a community that looks forward to co-creating a future together.

The most effective leaders have emotional and conversational intelligence while demonstrating empathy and humility. They know when, how and why to drive change and when to step back.

Know yourself, find your voice and speak with authority so others will listen.

Remember also the importance of listening and learning yourself. Engage your people and prioritize what you need to learn first and fastest. And always ask questions, it ensures you understand the subject matter and reinforces the fact you are interested in what is being said.

Likewise, encourage feedback on your planning and objectives. Feedback, both positive and negative will help build your decision-making – it means stakeholders are compelled to share their thoughts and can help you adjust your strategy to win across more people. Everyone likes feeling involved and at a time when you need advocates to deliver your plans, it's a great way to build champions.

For this reason, consider creating your stakeholder map of those individuals in the organization whom you need to work with, collaborate with and be visible in front of. Who do you need to engage with in order to get your message to the top?

Build your own performance development plan to focus you on your personal goals. Doing this at the start of a new role will focus you on defining your objectives and what success will look like, enabling you to develop a series of KPIs which you can continually track and report against. Within this plan, allow several metrics around your own continuous learning, and how you can develop your personal brand.

Monitor and report regularly on all of your key actions aligned with your gap analysis and job description. Track progress as you complete these initiatives and keep a record of performance against KPIs.

Keeping on top of your KPIs and managing expectations is essential – get to understand what the business expects of you and, in turn, make it clear, what you expect from your business and peers.

Egos are one of the biggest stumbling blocks for new directors and executives. Leave your ego behind and practice being humble and be willing to listen and learn.

Focus on your strengths and play to them every day but don't shy away from new challenges where you believe they will add value or exposure. Whilst it is important to push yourself and to develop a broad range of skills, learning on the job in a new role increases risk of failure and can build stress and anxiety.

Remember why you wanted the role in the first place and that in getting to this position you succeeded over a field of highly qualified peers. Focus on the skills that got you the role and the fact that you've been entrusted with delivering results for your boss and the business. They have put huge faith in you to deliver.

> Confidence is key – you are where you are because the business believes in your ability to deliver results. Your boss, CEO, board, shareholders and customers all want and need you to succeed.

Learn the language of confidence – your choice of words and delivery reflect your gravitas, confidence and credibility. The energy you bring to the job will directly impact upon the morale and motivation of the business – if you come across as nervous or uncertain, it can harm the whole company. Practice a short elevator pitch, detailing your latest projects and recent achievements – a concise and polished overview will demonstrate you are clear on your objectives and focused on results.

Feeling confident is directly related to looking the part and aligned with making a good impression, not just on day one but every day. As mentioned before, whilst a suit is usual business attire, business leaders have mastered appearance in all guises so as to reflect confidence and ability. What works for you and the business?

Learn how, what and why to promote yourself and your achievement. No one likes a show-off or arrogance, but if you're not visible you won't get the recognition you deserve – you risk not being front of mind in a busy organization and not getting the support you require for your vision and your projects.

And, finally don't forget to practice what you preach. Live your company culture and embody your vision so that you become a role model in the eyes of your team and peers.

MAINTAINING ONGOING CAREER MOMENTUM

"You were hired because you met expectations, you will be promoted if you can exceed them." Saji Ijiyemi

Business leaders are dealing with rapidly changing markets, technologies, workforces and increased financial and legal scrutiny.

Very few of us will ever have the opportunity to reach the very top of our profession.

Each career progression is made easier by building ongoing career momentum. If you rest on your laurels – drifting along out of sight – the momentum in the business will shift behind someone else.

At each stage of your career, as you move from manager to director and even C-Level so the challenges and pressures will grow, but at the same time, so will your exposure and network. Your skills will be refined, your specialist knowledge may decline, but your exposure across the business and industry will rise.

Having followed our guidance in this book and used your own common sense to apply what you've learnt, so you will find new opportunities to influence and progress in your personal development and expand your remit in the business.

We spoke earlier about planning a road map for your future career growth – this is an organic plan, evolving as your ambitions and objectives change. The important thing is to never lose track of what your objective is and to understand the plans the business has for you – and, more importantly, the extent of your own ambition.

The challenges of senior level leadership shouldn't be taken lightly. You will know you are ready to consider the next career move when you feel yourself growing in confidence and have the ability to relax into your role.

Consider how you shape other peoples opinions? How often do other people help shape your views? Have you grown your influence across the business?

Are you enjoying your role?

Are you thriving?

SECTION 5

BIG FIVE TIPS

1. Prepare thoroughly for the interview process when you have identified your next role – the other candidates (your competition) will!
2. Reframe the way you think and feel about any setbacks – it's not unusual to fail.
3. Commit and have a clear action orientated 90-day plan – focused on adding immediate value.
4. Work internal and external relationships fully – get people on your side.
5. Enjoy and thrive in your new role – it's what you wanted.

GLOSSARY

CEO – Chief Executive Officer

CTO – Chief Technology Officer

C-IQ – conversational IQ

CIO – Chief Information Officer

EI – emotional intelligence

SEO – search engine optimization

VC – video-conferencing

IM – instant messenger

Millennial – a person born after 1980

CV – curriculum vitae, also known as a resume

P&L – profit and loss statement

KPI – key performance indicator

REFERENCES

Right Management Report
http://www.manpowergroup.com/wps/wcm/connect/manpowergroup-en/home/newsroom/news-releases/2013/right+management+global+survey+reports+most+employee+engagement+misses+the+mark+in+driving+business+goals

Director Magazine Survey
http://www.director.co.uk/MAGAZINE/2010/10_November/director-rewards-survey_64_03.html

Want To Be A CEO? Stay Put – Wendy Todaro
http://www.forbes.com/2003/03/31/cx_wt_0401exec.html

We Wait Too Long to Train Our Leaders – Jack Zenger
http://blogs.hbr.org/2012/12/why-do-we-wait-so-long-to-trai/

Does age matter when you're CEO?
http://usatoday30.usatoday.com/money/companies/management/2008-08-12-obama-mccain-age-ceos_N.htm

Corporate Directors Get Older, Hold Their Seats Longer – Carol Hymowitz
http://www.businessweek.com/articles/2013-05-23/corporate-directors-get-older-hold-their-seats-longer

Five Reasons We're Losing A Whole Generation of Managers – Kristi Hedges
http://www.forbes.com/sites/work-in-progress/2013/01/16/five-reasons-were-losing-a-whole-generation-of-managers/

The 2014 FD Salary Survey – Richard Crump, Rachael Singh
http://www.financialdirector.co.uk/financial-director/special/2322799/the-2014-fd-salary-survey

Average 36-year wait to progress to FTSE 100 board member – Hannah Uttley
http://www.wsandb.co.uk/wsb/news/2280608/average-36-year-wait-to-progress-to-ftse-100-board-member

ILM Research Paper 3 – Manager profile
https://www.i-l-m.com/~/media/ILM%20Website/Downloads/Insight/Reports_from_ILM_website/uk-managers-profile-2013%20pdf.ashx

Procter & Gamble's nurture culture
http://www.the-chiefexecutive.com/features/featureceo-procter-gamble-talent/

The Talent Perspective: What does it feel like to be talent-managed? – http://www.cipd.co.uk/NR/rdonlyres/95D2D604-36C6-450A-996A-01F45F0B17C5/0/5262_Talent_Perspective.pdf

Worldwide, 13% of Employees Are Engaged at Work – Steve Crabtree
http://www.gallup.com/poll/165269/worldwide-employees-engaged-work.aspx

Why Companies Fail To Engage Today's Workforce: The Overwhelmed Employee – Josh Bersin
http://www.forbes.com/sites/joshbersin/2014/03/15/why-companies-fail-to-engage-todays-workforce-the-overwhelmed-employee/

Your Employees Want the Negative Feedback You Hate to Give – Jack Zenger, Joseph Folkman
https://hbr.org/2014/01/your-employees-want-the-negative-feedback-you-hate-to-give/

You only get one chance to create a great first impression – Dean Williams
https://www.yourreadybusiness.co.uk/you-only-get-one-chance-to-create-a-great-first-impression/

Improving A Leading Indicator of Financial Performance: Employee Engagement – Ty Kiisel
http://www.forbes.com/sites/alanhall/2013/03/11/im-outta-here-why-2-million-americans-quit-every-month-and-5-steps-to-turn-the-epidemic-around/

Why Men Still Get More Promotions Than Women
https://hbr.org/2010/09/why-men-still-get-more-promotions-than-women

2008 Catalyst Census Of Women Board Directors Of The Fortune 500
http://www.catalyst.org/knowledge/2008-catalyst-census-women-board-directors-fortune-500

18 Statistics to Help Convince Your CEO to Engage
https://www.impactbnd.com/blog/18-statistics-to-help-convince-your-ceo-to-engage

How social technologies drive business success.
http://www.millwardbrown.com/docs/default-source/insight-documents/articles-and-reports/Googe_MillwardBrown_How-Social-Technologies-Drive-Business-Success_201205.pdf

2012 Edelman Trust Barometer
http://www.edelman.com/insights/intellectual-property/2012-edelman-trust-barometer/

The Most Unusual Interview Questions, And How To Answer Them – Bernard Marr
https://www.linkedin.com/pulse/20140804100911-64875646-the-most-unusual-interview-questions-and-how-to-answer-them

What Got You Here, Won't Get You There: How successful people become even more successful – Marshall Goldsmith

Lightning Source UK Ltd.
Milton Keynes UK
UKOW05f0633200617
303732UK00001B/249/P

9 781786 238030